New Directions for
Child and Adolescent
Development

Reed W. Larson
Lene Arnett Jensen
EDITORS-IN-CHIEF

William Damon
FOUNDING EDITOR

Social Interaction and the Development of Executive Function

Charlie Lewis
Jeremy I. M. Carpendale
EDITORS

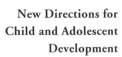

Number 123 • Spring 2009
Jossey-Bass
San Francisco

SOCIAL INTERACTION AND THE DEVELOPMENT OF EXECUTIVE FUNCTION
Charlie Lewis, Jeremy I. M. Carpendale (eds.)
New Directions for Child and Adolescent Development, no. 123
Reed W. Larson, Lene Arnett Jensen, Editors-in-Chief

© 2009 Wiley Periodicals, Inc., A Wiley Company. All rights reserved.

No part of this publication may be reproduced, stored in a retrieval system, or transmitted in any form or by any means, electronic, mechanical, photocopying, recording, scanning, or otherwise, except as permitted under Sections 107 or 108 of the 1976 United States Copyright Act, without either the prior written permission of the Publisher or authorization through payment of the appropriate per-copy fee to the Copyright Clearance Center, 222 Rosewood Drive, Danvers, MA 01923; (978) 750-8400, fax (978) 646-8600. Requests to the Publisher for permission should be addressed to the Permissions Department, John Wiley & Sons, Inc., 111 River St., Hoboken, NJ 07030, (201) 748-6011, fax (201) 748-6008, www.wiley.com/go/permissions.

Microfilm copies of issues and articles are available in 16mm and 35mm, as well as microfiche in 105mm, through University Microfilms, Inc., 300 North Zeeb Road, Ann Arbor, Michigan 48106-1346.

ISSN 1520-3247   electronic ISSN 1534-8687

NEW DIRECTIONS FOR CHILD AND ADOLESCENT DEVELOPMENT is part of The Jossey-Bass Education Series and is published quarterly by Wiley Subscription Services, Inc., a Wiley company, at Jossey-Bass, 989 Market Street, San Francisco, California 94103-1741. Periodicals postage paid at San Francisco, California, and at additional mailing offices. Postmaster: Send address changes to New Directions for Child and Adolescent Development, Jossey-Bass, 989 Market Street, San Francisco, CA 94103-1741.

New Directions for Child and Adolescent Development is indexed in Cambridge Scientific Abstracts (CSA/CIG), CHID: Combined Health Information Database (NIH), Contents Pages in Education (T&F), Current Abstracts (EBSCO), Educational Research Abstracts Online (T&F), ERIC Database (Education Resources Information Center), Index Medicus/MEDLINE/PubMed (NLM), Linguistics & Language Behavior Abstracts (CSA/CIG), Psychological Abstracts/PsycINFO (APA), Social Services Abstracts (CSA/CIG), SocINDEX (EBSCO), and Sociological Abstracts (CSA/CIG).

SUBSCRIPTION rates: For the U.S., $85 for individuals and $280 for institutions. Please see ordering information page at end of journal.

EDITORIAL CORRESPONDENCE should be e-mailed to the editors-in-chief: Reed W. Larson (larsonr@uiuc.edu) and Lene Arnett Jensen (ljensen@clarku.edu).

Jossey-Bass Web address: www.josseybass.com

Contents

1. Introduction: Links Between Social Interaction and Executive Function — 1
   Charlie Lewis, Jeremy I. M. Carpendale
   This chapter introduces the study of executive function and theoretical perspectives acknowledging the influence of social interaction and outlines the contributions made by the chapters in this volume.

2. Parental Scaffolding and the Development of Executive Function — 17
   Maximilian B. Bibok, Jeremy I. M. Carpendale, Ulrich Müller
   In this chapter the authors take a microgenetic approach to illustrating the role of parental scaffolding in development of executive function.

3. How Do Families Help or Hinder the Emergence of Early Executive Function? — 35
   Claire H. Hughes, Rosie A. Ensor
   A longitudinal study of a socially diverse group of families, reported in this chapter, examines the links between aspects of family interaction and development of executive function.

4. New Directions in Evaluating Social Problem Solving in Childhood: Early Precursors and Links to Adolescent Social Competence — 51
   Susan H. Landry, Karen E. Smith, Paul R. Swank
   This chapter presents an ecologically valid measure of social problem solving that is linked to earlier development and that predicts social interactive skills in early adolescence.

5. Culture, Executive Function, and Social Understanding — 69
   Charlie Lewis, Masuo Koyasu, Seungmi Oh, Ayako Ogawa, Benjamin Short, Zhao Huang
   This chapter examines differences in the links between executive function and social understanding in four cultures in order to question current assumptions about their relationship.

6. Social Origins of Executive Function Development — 87
   Stephanie M. Carlson
   This final chapter is an integrative commentary on the chapters in this volume, setting the discussion in the context of other recent research and suggesting new directions for research on the social origins of executive function.

INDEX — 99

Lewis, C., & Carpendale, J. I. M. (2009). Introduction: Links between social interaction and executive function. In C. Lewis & J. I. M. Carpendale (Eds.), Social interaction and the development of executive function. *New Directions in Child and Adolescent Development, 123*, 1–15.

1

Introduction: Links Between Social Interaction and Executive Function

Charlie Lewis, Jeremy I. M. Carpendale

Abstract

The term executive function is used increasingly within developmental psychology and is often taken to refer to unfolding brain processes. We trace the origins of research on executive function to show that the link with social interaction has a long history. We suggest that a recent frenzy of research exploring methods for studying individual executive skills should pay more attention to the tradition exploring the role of social interaction in their development. © Wiley Periodicals, Inc.

> *Inhibition* is therefore a history of the relation, as embodied in language, between specialized claims about nature and social values. There has indeed been a common discourse over the last two centuries or so for the science and morality of control within the individual person and in political economy
> —Smith (1992), p. 228, his emphasis

Psychologists in the past 20 years have homed in on a group of skills that control our actions and thoughts, under the banner "executive function." The cognitive "revolution" of the 1950s was heralded in books such as Broadbent's *Perception and Communication* (1958); it presented a psychology in which the aim was to study the flow of information from the sense organs to the individual's response. This information-processing approach came under revision in the 1970s and 1980s with the inclusion of supervisory systems that regulate the flow of information and control behavior, as we see, for example, in the working-memory model of Baddeley and Hitch (1974; Baddeley, 1886) or Norman and Shallice's Supervisory Activating System (1980). Such control mechanisms have become central to the make-up of executive function and refer to a number of interrelated skills.

We briefly describe these skills here. First, *working memory* refers to the capacity not only to hold information in mind but to be able to report it in a way that is not simply rote repetition. *Attentional flexibility* or "set shifting" is the ability to change from one way of solving a problem to another complementary means. *Inhibitory control* refers to the propensity to suppress prepotent responses, as in hurrying to copy an adult even if he or she has not prefaced an instruction, in the popular game, with "Simon says." *Planning* is often taken to be the superordinate executive skill because to perform complex actions such as completing a shopping trip or cooking a complex meal involves a combination of all these skills.

Increasingly the topic of executive function has been explored in terms of its neural correlates and is seen by some as a new way of examining the higher levels of cognitive processing. Yet, rather than being the new kids on the block, these constructs have a long tradition, one that is not well documented in the history of psychology. A cursory look at this history is sufficient to show that executive function has been eminent in psychology, with the roles of cognition and social interactions identified as intertwined. For a start, concepts such as inhibition and control were repeatedly used in the study of the mind long before Freud focused on mental processes that constrain our natural impulses. Roger Smith's detailed and fascinating history of one strand of executive function, inhibition, shows that over the 19th century the term originated in moral debate about the control of behavior, gradually filtering into discussion in neurophysiology from the 1830s and into development of psychology in the late 19th century. Smith (1992, pp. 68–69) shows that even early analyses of the reflex, published in the 1830s, focused on a "higher" regulatory system for control of behavior. He also points out that executive processes are discussed at length in William James's *Principles of Psychology* (1890). Smith's history is important because he shows the continuing fault lines in constructs such as inhibition that can be extended to all areas of executive function. These issues concern the relative roles of social processes, social learning, and physiological processes in development of control and the nature of the executive system itself.

The authors in this volume represent a continuing strand of studies attempting to bridge the gap between social interaction and executive function, and thus to get a better grasp of how the two constructs relate to each other. In this chapter we briefly present an analysis of the origins of current work exploring the role of social factors in executive function. The first main section examines the theoretical debate we feel has informed such recent analyses but not been given pride of place in them. The second part explores some key methodological issues, to address how we measure executive skills in children and how our measurements might be improved. In the final and briefest section, we attempt to situate the chapters in this volume in terms of our theoretical and methodological analyses.

Theorizing the Links Between Social Interaction and Executive Function

Interest in development of executive function has primarily taken a neuropsychological perspective, but researchers in this new wave of research are beginning to consider the possible role of social interaction in such development. This is actually a return to the view emphasized by a researcher whose pioneering work on conceptualization, measurement, and remediation of executive functions has had a major influence on contemporary research, Alexander Luria (e.g., 1961). The reason we start this introduction with a reference to a longer history is that Luria drew on a tradition of theory in which a central issue was the role of social processes in executive skills. In the early 20th century, there was much discussion about the evolutionary function of executive skills. Mead (1910, p. 178) suggested that "human conduct is distinguished primarily from animal conduct by that increase in inhibition which is an essential phase of voluntary attention, and increased inhibition means an increase in gesture in the signs of activities which are not carried out; in the assumptions of attitudes whose values in conduct fail to get complete expression." A similar point was made by Vygotsky (1978, p. 28).

Indeed, it is Vygotsky's theory that we believe has informed the thinking behind the research reported in this book and the theoretical implications of this work, although his influence remains somewhat hidden in contemporary debate. Like Mead, Vygotsky characterized intelligent human activity as the ability to deliberate between alternative response actions. Such skill requires the person to distance herself or himself from the types of immediate reaction to the world that are seen in animals or in people who make "unthinking" prepotent responses. Language and related symbol systems, learned and maintained through social interaction, are central to the process of gaining self-control via what Vygotsky (1978) terms "higher" cognitive processes, notably planning, memory, and inhibition.

Thus for Vygotsky development of executive function is a natural consequence of social learning. Simple actions such as tying a knot in one's handkerchief or making a shopping list transform biologically given skills such as "natural memory" into more versatile higher functions that are mediated by signs. Thus social interactions and social conventions drive cognitive development and link the individual into historical and cultural traditions. This "permits humans, by the aid of extrinsic stimuli, *to control their behaviour from the outside*. The use of signs leads humans to a specific structure of behaviour that breaks away from biological development and creates new forms of a culturally-based psychological process" (Vygotsky, 1978, p. 40, emphasis in original). The lesson of Vygotsky's theory is that it is a mistake to consider executive processes in isolation from the individual's psychosocial functioning. As Luria (1981, p. 89) put it: "We must go beyond the limits of the individual organism and examine how volitional processes are formed for the child in his/her concrete contacts with adults. . . . The source of the volitional act is the child's communication with adults. . . . The volitional act: not initially a mental act, not a simple habit: rather it is mediated by speech."

More systematic historical research is needed, but it is clear that an initial interest in developmental research on the Vygotsky-Luria hypothesis following its introduction to the West did not receive complete support. Miller, Shelton, and Flavell (1970) did not find support for Luria's claims that speech helps the child regulate her behavior. Other research produced more positive evidence, particularly that of Walter Mischel and Ignatius Toner in two series of studies on the role of arousal and motivation toward delay of gratification. In Mischel's work, children could delay gratification if they reflected on suppressing the temptation, rather than focusing on performance of the task (Patterson & Mischel, 1976) or if asked to imagine a reward as something else (e.g., Mischel & Baker, 1975). Toner explored the effects of children's motivation in another delay-of-gratification procedure (Ritchie & Toner, 1984; Toner, Moore, & Emmons, 1980; Toner & Smith, 1977). Before the task, the experimenter said to the preschooler either that he had heard the child was, for example, patient (a task-relevant remark) or that she had a lot of friends in the preschool (a task-irrelevant remark). The assessment involved how long it would take the child to grab for candies that were designated as the child's and whose pile was added to every 30 seconds. Toner found that children in the group in which the experimenter made a task-relevant remark waited significantly longer to claim the candies allocated to them and therefore obtained a larger reward. This effect was obtained even when one experimenter made the remark and a second experimenter, unaware of which remark had been made to the child, administered the delay-of-gratification task.

This work on delay of gratification shows the roles of social interaction and the child's motivation in development and use of executive skills. Research exploring development of self-regulation, or how children gain control over their behavior, has carried on the social interaction tradition and merged it with others. It has assumed that this developmental process starts with the interactions between children and their caregivers (Kopp, 1982; Rothbart & Derryberry, 1981). This term emerged as a result of research showing that toddlers between one and two years old become aware of the demands on social control that are negotiated with their parents. A recent meta-analysis shows there is a gradual transfer from external to internal processes that can be seen within the framework of developing attachments (Karreman, van Tuijl, van Aken, & Dekovi, 2006).

These strands of research, on delay of gratification and self-regulation, have maintained a trickle of interest in the role of social interaction in self-control. However, we think it is fair to suggest that as work on executive function progressed it became less social and more individualistic and located purely within neuropsychological pathways (e.g., Aron, 2008). This is partly due to development of procedures for measuring neurological activity, such as MRI and PET (used primarily with adults) and EEG. These techniques suggest that executive skills are located in specific areas of the brain, particularly in the frontal lobes, and are revealing interesting separations and links (e.g., Knight & Stuss, 2002). Second, as Zelazo, Müller, Frye, and Marcovitch (2003) point out, a majority of the research on executive functions over the past two decades has adopted what they term an "empirical" approach in which the focus of attention is on devising a test for one of the component skills of executive function. For example, Gerstadt, Hong, and Diamond (1994) constructed a measure called the Day-Night task to assess the construct of inhibition discussed at the start of the chapter. Children were presented with a series of pictures of the sun on a white background or the moon or stars on a black card. Participants had to say "day" to the moon and "night" as soon as a card with the sun was revealed. In keeping with the idea that children gain increasing inhibitory control over the preschool years, Gerstadt and colleagues found a sharp rise in the ability to resist the temptation to label the tasks in keeping with picture of the card (i.e., "day" to the sun), which they attributed to developments in the connections made in the prefrontal cortex. However, they also reported that social interactional factors influenced the performance of children. Those in day care did better than those raised exclusively at home, suggesting that something about extrafamilial care and a greater number of peer interactions might facilitate the rate of acquisition of key executive skills. Since that study, other social correlates with executive skills have been identified, particularly socioeconomic status (e.g., Ardila, Roselli, Matute, & Guajardo, 2005; Noble, McCandliss, & Farah, 2007), but in the main such links have been overlooked.

In this section, we have argued that the social basis of executive function receives less attention than one might expect given the historical backdrop of research from Luria and Vygotsky (Zelazo et al., 2003). Theoretical analyses in keeping with that tradition, such as that of Zelazo and Jacques (1996), became the exception rather than the rule. Although this has changed very recently (Fernyhough, in press; Landry & Smith, in press; Lewis, Carpendale, Towse, & Maridaki-Kassotaki, in press; Sokol & Müller, 2007), we see the theoretical issues raised in this volume as a resurgence of the Vygotsky-Luria tradition, rather than as a continuation of the tradition inspired by the trickle of work described here. We turn now to more recent preoccupations.

Methodological Issues in Analysis of Executive Function

The main impetus behind the recent phase of research into development of executive function has come from within the "cognitive revolution's" attempt to understand the mind-brain system. No doubt this tradition will develop apace in the coming years, but we discuss here the grounds for maintaining the dimension of social interaction within models of the development and nature of these skills.

Much of the recent work has explored the cognitive architecture of the executive system to determine whether we can distinguish between individual skills that make up that system. In recent years there has been some consolidation of evidence and theory on the topic. An influential paper by Akira Miyake and his colleagues (Miyake, Friedman, Emerson, Witzki, Howerter, & Wager, 2000) examined whether and how the components of executive function fit together, using structural equation modeling to find the best way of relating each component to the others. In adults they found that the individual skills described at the start of the chapter (working memory, attentional flexibility, and inhibitory control; they use other terms but we use these to be consistent with the literature in developmental psychology) should be treated as separate entities, but the best model was one in which they all fit together into a superordinate construct "executive function," including planning. They termed this a "unity-with-diversity" model, as each individual variable was distinct but needed to be correlated with the others.

Miyake et al.'s model (2000) was constructed on large amounts of data collected from adults. They have since shown a high level of stability between childhood and adolescence (Friedman et al., 2007), and an even higher heritability of adult executive functioning was identified in an adult-twin study (Friedman, Miyake, Young, DeFries, Corley, & Hewitt, in press). However, we must be cautious about generalizing from these relatively stable data in adults to executive function in children; nor should we simply assume that there is an equivalence between adult and child executive skills, or that the latter develop within a social vacuum. We examine each of these issues in turn.

How well do definitions of executive function derived from research on adults transfer to children? One study of older children (Lehto, Juujarvi, Kooistra, & Pulkkinen, 2003) echoed Miyake's findings (2000) in terms of a unified system of skills in working memory, attentional flexibility, and inhibitory control. Yet Huizinga, Dolan, and van der Molen (2006) failed to find that measures of inhibition in children were related to other executive skills. So the jury is still out on whether there are commonalities between adults' and children's executive skills. Such differences reveal further issues and potential problems. For a start, simply assuming that tests are measures of only one construct is not sufficient, particularly when examining measures designed to be child-friendly. Discussion of what is referred to as "task impurity" (e.g., Rabbitt, 1997) suggests that tasks designed to test one construct often necessarily involve other abilities. For example, tests of inhibitory control and set shifting almost necessarily involve a degree of working memory, as the child has to recall which responses to make and which to inhibit. The Day-Night test (Gerstadt, Hong, & Diamond, 1994), described earlier, contains a control condition that, in theory, allows researchers to extract the effect of extraneous working memory skills, as it involves recalling the two words *day* and *night* arbitrarily assigned to one of two abstract patterns. Yet researchers usually pay little attention to these conditions. Our attempt to do so suggests a close correspondence between the Day-Night pictures and the versions with two abstract patterns, thus suggesting that the latter does not simply take out the working memory component of the former (Lewis, Solis-Trapala, Shimmon, & Diggle, in progress; Shimmon, 2005). Furthermore, attempts to measure test-retest reliability (Bishop, Aadmodt-Leeper, Cresswell, McGurk, & Skuse, 2001) and the correspondence between related tests (Bull, Espy, & Senn, 2004) have been low, thus leading to questions about the consistency of children's performance, at least in terms of more complex executive tasks involving planning. We explore individual tasks in the rest of this section.

First, we feel that these issues concerning test construction and reliability raise more fundamental questions about the nature of executive skills and how we measure them. If these skills are about continuous processes (such as keeping something in mind, anticipating a need to change a response to environmental stimuli, or inhibiting the desire to open the cookie jar), then we should consider thinking about the psychological dimension of such skills dynamically and designing measures that tap into such dynamics. As Zelazo and Müller (2002) note, a construct such as inhibition does not specify how the process of inhibition is selected and used by the individual. Let us look at the second issue first.

How can we tap into the dynamics of executive processes? Towse, Lewis, and Knowles (2007) considered this question in relation to a phenomenon common to both young children and the elderly, concerning the struggle with remembering to follow an action in response to an anticipated prompt. We modified a paradigm known as goal neglect (Duncan, Emslie,

Williams, Johnson, & Freer, 1996) in which children had to identify food items that appear every few seconds in two houses identified as a target by a cue (e.g., an arrow) as to which house to identify the items in. The children knew there would be a second cue (e.g., a blue or red square to identify the color of the house) to indicate whether to keep naming the food items in the same house or switch to naming them in the second. Participants also were assessed on a test of set shifting and a measure of inhibitory control. Two findings are relevant here. First, the two cues related differentially to the other executive tests. Responses to the first cue (the ability to follow a simple command) were correlated with the measure of conflict inhibition (a test like the Day-Night task), while the second cue correlated with set shifting as measured by the Dimension Change Card Sort (DCCS; Frye, Zelazo, & Palfai, 1995; see below), in which the child has to sort a series of cards by color and then sort them by shape (or vice versa). This suggests that there is some mileage in considering children's performance by examining the dynamics of test performance (Towse et al., 2007).

Second, the type of cue used to direct children's attention influenced their compliance. Participants made more errors in response to a color cue than an arrow, presumably because the arrow is more directive. These data suggest that the child's executive functions can be directed by "external" influences, which raises the question of how extensive these external conditions are. Indeed, the findings lead to two possible ways by which such cues influence the child's self-regulation, and both tie into Vygotsky's theory: the role of others in guiding the child into areas of self-controlled activity and the part played by symbolic processes in higher-level mental functions.

Despite a shift in focus over the past quarter century toward the nature of tests of executive skills, the recent research described here keeps leading us back to a more socially embedded perspective. The DCCS task is a good example. In this procedure, children are asked to sort cards, differentiated by shape and color, into one of two trays. After six sorts, the sorting criteria are changed (from color to shape or vice versa). Three-year-olds typically continue to sort cards by the first (preswitch) rule, even if only one or two preswitch trials are performed (Frye et al., 1995). Indeed, responses tend to be bimodal, suggesting that children either get the rule or do not. Frye et al. interpret these findings as suggesting that young children's failure on this task and older children's success can be attributed to development of an ability to construct higher-order rules that make up two rule systems (e.g., the shape and color rule sets) accessible to conscious control. This is known as Cognitive Complexity and Control (CCC) theory.

The DCCS procedure has been replicated many times (see Zelazo et al., 2003, for a recent summary of theory and data), and the CCC theory is open to the possibility that the child gains an understanding of the higher-order rules through social interaction. However, the theory is not without its detractors (e.g., Kirkham, Cruess, & Diamond, 2003; Munakata & Yerys,

2001), some of whom propose more socially embedded explanations for the developmental shifts seen between the ages of three and four. Three studies, for example, emphasize the interaction between child and experimenter in managing the child's performance. The first, by Towse et al. (2000), suggested that if three-year-olds are given more support to understand the postswitch rules (explained in the same way that the preswitch rules were), their level of performance improved greatly. Likewise, Brace, Morton, and Munakata (2006) found that demonstrating the correct response was more successful than giving the standard instruction, suggesting that something about the experimenter-child interaction scaffolds the child's activity, in some circumstances facilitating successful performance.

Perhaps the clearest recent demonstration of the effects of social interaction on the DCCS performance of three-year-olds comes from a series of four experiments published by Moriguchi, Lee, and Itakura (2007). Previous work had found no effect of placing the DCCS task into an interactive context. For example, Jacques, Zelazo, Kirkham, and Semcesen (1999) had found that three-year-olds were inaccurate in their judgments of a puppet's successful or unsuccessful performance in the postswitch trials. In Moriguchi et al., witnessing an adult model making errors on the preswitch trials led to children making fewer errors while following the same rule on the postswitch trials themselves. So the correct strategy was to use the sorting strategy they had not seen being used. They manipulated the procedure to test whether there was an effect of the actor expressing awareness of errors or confidence in performance. Moriguchi and colleagues found that these social factors had a dramatic influence on performance. So, having sorted the cards incorrectly, if the actor says she was right in her sorting then almost 80% of three-year-olds failed, while if the actor says she made a mistake or is not sure then 80% of three-year-olds' performance jumped to a ceiling level. This study is a timely reminder of the potential influence of social interactions on children's performance in executive tasks. Interestingly, it has a resonance with a series of Russian studies in the Vygotsky-Luria tradition that have not been translated into English (e.g., Subbotsky, 1976). In one such study, when a child performs a version of Luria's hand game with an experimenter and an adult confederate, if the confederate performs the wrong gesture a majority of five-year-olds will err by copying him even though most will succeed when doing the task without the confederate present.

How do these social interaction processes influence children's executive skills? The three manipulations of the DCCS just discussed share a structure in which the adult scaffolds the child's performance, but we need to explore how this works. A Vygotskian interpretation would hold that the interaction between adult and child permits the latter to gain some symbolic mastery, and therefore control, over his or her actions. The DCCS does not easily lend itself to manipulations, which allow exploration of the effect of symbolic representation on preschoolers' understanding. However, there is a collection of tasks examining the child's ability to inhibit a prepotent response that facilitates such manipulations. Often termed conflict inhibition, in these tasks the child has to choose the less rewarding stimulus in order to receive the greater reward. For example, in Carlson, Davis, and Leach's procedure (2005) the child needs to point to the smaller number of treats in order to receive the larger number when two alternatives are presented. Three-year-olds have a problem either pressing a button before reaching into a box for a treat (Hughes & Russell, 1993) or pointing to an empty box when there is another with a candy in it (Russell, Mauthner, Sharpe, & Tidswell, 1991). What happens when the task involves a symbolic cue to guide children to an understanding of the task?

Carlson et al. (2005, experiment 2) gave children a task in which they could win two candies or five. In one condition the candies were on the top of a box, while in three other conditions they were concealed inside the boxes, with a symbolic representation on the top of each to represent the contents: two or five stones, a few or many dots, or a mouse and an elephant to represent the number of sweets inside. Interestingly, Carlson et al. found that the mouse-elephant condition led to greatest success (significantly more than the real-treat condition) and in this and the dots conditions children were significantly above chance. The overall findings suggested that use of symbolic moderation can help preschoolers give a correct answer, presumably because the symbol allows or forces them to distance themselves from the reward. These findings are in keeping with similar experiments in which children use a symbol such as a model pointing hand to identify the box without a reward, in the Windows Task (Hala & Russell, 2001).

Increasing the Focus on Social Interaction and Executive Function

To summarize our analysis thus far: research on development of executive skills was based on a tradition that assumes such skills are embedded in social processes, but this tradition has been somewhat sidelined as researchers become increasingly focused on measurement of the components of executive function and their possible relation to neurological pathways. The aim of this volume is to present some current research that highlights the resurgence of an approach to the topic that takes social interactions and social relationships as the starting point. What follows is a selection of four chapters and a discussion attempting to home in on different aspects of the social interaction–executive function relationship in an attempt to draw the reader's attention to its complexity rather than furnish definitive answers.

In this volume, we start off with an examination of the dyad and move continuously outward, in part across the span of childhood but mainly in terms of the range of factors that influence social interaction. Despite considerable differences among individual chapters, a common theme concerns the role of executive function in the child's negotiation of and learning within social interactions.

The focus of Bibok, Carpendale, and Müller's chapter is the dyadic interactions between two-year-olds and their caregivers. Although they concentrate on the nature of parental scaffolding as defined by David Wood and his colleagues, this chapter is an attempt to show that such interactions are far more complex; the effectiveness of parents' attempts to structure the child's cognitive performance is itself in part determined by the child's ability to decipher and contribute to them. Bibok and colleagues take a very close look at the "social structure of scaffolding" to show the complexities of the relationship between social interactions and the child's executive skills, even very early in her or his development.

The focus on scaffolding is broadened even further by Hughes and Ensor, who set out to show that adult-child interactions are only "part of the jigsaw." They point out that the study of social interactions is not incompatible with more biological approaches and even genetic analyses, as long as our interpretation of each is sufficiently flexible. Hughes and Ensor focus on the distinction between the child's direct interactions and the factors that might influence those interactions, notably the family's socioeconomic status and domestic environment. They stress the role of separating executive function from other general cognitive skills such as the child's language level. They show that we need to go beyond the parents' direct scaffolding of their children's skills to understand the contextual influences on them, including the relative "chaos" in the family environment.

Three of the chapters focus exclusively on preschool children. The exception is that of Landry, Smith, and Swank. They use age eight as a pivot around which they consider predictors from the preschool period and sequelae in the children's social functioning in adolescence. The central focus is on developing a measure of social problem solving in eight-year-olds that is ecologically valid and goes beyond reliance on parental report on the social-cognitive skills in middle childhood. They show that social problem solving is predicted by factors in the child's preschool skills and is predictive of their social interactive skills at age 13. Data from Landry et al. clearly show the continuing interplay among social, executive, and general cognitive processes throughout the course of development.

The final data-based chapter extends the focus from social and developmental processes to analyze the role of culture in determining the link between social interactions and executive function. A spate of recent studies has shown that oriental children seem to have highly advanced executive skills, such as working memory (Tardif, So, & Kaciroti, 2007) and conflict inhibition (Sabbagh, Xu, Carlson, Moses, & Lee, 2006). In their chapter, Lewis, Koyasu, Oh, Ogawa, Short, and Huang consider this precocious development in terms of two prevailing sets of findings, an apparent pan-cultural link between executive function and social understanding, and associations between family relationships and both these factors. Not only is an understanding of cultural processes crucial to our understanding of factors such as a precocious executive functioning, Lewis et al. claim that cross-cultural research can be used to question prevailing Western assumptions about the development of executive skills.

In the final chapter, Stephanie Carlson draws the volume to a close by placing the preceding chapters into a broader theoretical context. She returns to the issue of how we can and should consider the complexity of the term *social interaction* by examining the trade-off between proximal and distal factors. To do this, Carlson turns, like us, to historical analyses and homes in on the work of George Herbert Mead as a means of understanding the motivational factors underlying self-regulation. The aim of this volume is not to dismiss the explosion of recent work into the neural structure and function of executive processes. Carlson's conclusion is a fitting one for her chapter, this one, and the volume as a whole: a complete grasp of executive function and its development will lie in an approach with multiple levels, from social processes down to the neurophysiological. Such an enterprise will heal some of the rifts that were in evidence 200 years ago when terms such as inhibition and executive control entered into debates about the control of human conduct (Smith, 1992).

References

Appleton, M., & Reddy, V. (1996). Teaching three year-olds to pass false belief tests: A conversational approach. *Social Development, 5*, 275–291.
Ardila, A., Roselli, M., Matute, E., & Guajardo, S. (2005). The influence of parents' educational level on the development of executive functions. *Developmental Neuropsychology, 28*, 539–560.
Aron, A. R. (2008). Progress in executive function research: From tasks to functions to regions to networks. *Current Directions in Psychological Science, 17*, 124–129.
Astington, J. W., & Baird, J. A. (Eds.). (2005). *Why language matters for theory of mind.* New York: Oxford University Press.
Baddeley, A. D. (1986). *Working memory.* Oxford: Oxford University Press.
Baddeley, A. D., & Hitch, G. J. (1974). Working memory. In G. H. Bower (Ed.), *The psychology of learning and motivation, Vol. 8* (pp. 47–89). New York: Academic Press.
Bell, R. Q. (1968). A reinterpretation of the direction of effects in studies of socialization. *Psychological Review, 75*, 81–95.
Bishop, D.V.M., Aadmodt-Leeper, G., Cresswell, C., McGurk, R., & Skuse, D. (2001). Individual differences in cognitive planning on the Tower of Hanoi task: Neuropsychological maturity or measurement error? *Journal of Child Psychology and Psychiatry, 42*, 551–556.
Brace, J. J., Morton, B. J., & Munakata, Y. (2006). When actions speak louder than words: Improving children's performance on a card-sorting task. *Psychological Science, 17*, 665–669.
Broadbent, D. E. (1958) *Perception and Communication.* London: Pergamon.
Bronfenbrenner, U. (1979). *The ecology of human development.* Cambridge, MA: Harvard University Press.
Bull, R., Espy, K. A., & Senn, T. E. (2004). A comparison of performance on the Towers of London and Hanoi in young children. *Journal of Child Psychology & Psychiatry, 45*, 743–754.

Carlson, S. M., Davis, A. C., & Leach, J. G. (2005). Less is more: Executive function and symbolic representation in preschool children. *Psychological Science, 16,* 609–616.

Duncan, J., Emslie, H., Williams, P., Johnson, R., & Freer, C. (1996). Intelligence and the frontal lobe: The organisation of goal directed behavior. *Cognitive Psychology, 30,* 257–303.

Fernyhough, C. (in press). Mediated cognition and social understanding. In B. Sokol, U. Müller, J. I. M. Carpendale, A. Young, & G. Iarocci (Eds.), *Self- and social-regulation: Exploring the relations between social interaction, social cognition, and the development of executive functions.* Oxford: Oxford University Press.

Friedman, N. P., et al. (2007). Greater attention problems during childhood predict poorer executive functions in late adolescence. *Psychological Science, 18,* 893–900.

Friedman, N. P., Miyake, A., Young, S. E., DeFries, J. C., Corley, R. P., & Hewitt, J. K. (in press). Individual differences in executive functions are almost entirely genetic in origin. *Journal of Experimental Psychology: General.*

Frye, D., Zelazo, P. D., & Palfai, T. (1995). Inference and action in early causal reasoning. *Cognitive Development, 10,* 120–131.

Gerstadt, C. L., Hong, Y. J., & Diamond, A. (1994). The relationship between cognition and action—performance of children 3 1/2–7 years old on a stroop-like day-night test. *Cognition, 53,* 129–153.

Hala, S., & Russell, J. (2001). Executive control within strategic deception: A window on early cognitive development? *Journal of Experimental Child Psychology, 80,* 112–141.

Hughes, C., & Russell, J. (1993). Autistic children's difficulty with mental disengagement from an object: Its implications for theories of autism. *Developmental Psychology, 29,* 498–510.

Huizinga, M., Dolan, C. V., & van der Molen, M. W. (2006). Age-related change in executive function: Developmental trends and a latent variable analysis. *Neuropsychologia, 44,* 2017–2036.

Jacques, S., Zelazo, P. D., Kirkham, N. Z., & Semcesen, T. K. (1999). Rule selection versus rule execution in preschoolers: An error-detection approach. *Developmental Psychology, 35,* 770–780.

James, William. (1890). *Principles of Psychology.* New York: Henry Holt.

Karreman, A., van Tuijl, C., van Aken, M.A.G., & Dekovi, M. (2006). Parenting and self-regulation: A meta-analysis. *Infant & Child Development, 15,* 561–579.

Kirkham, N. Z., Cruess, L., & Diamond, A. (2003). Helping children apply their knowledge to their behavior on a dimension-switching task. *Developmental Science, 6,* 449–467.

Knight, R. K., & Stuss, D. T. (Eds.). (2002). *Principles of frontal lobe function.* Oxford: Oxford University Press.

Kopp, C. (1982). Antecedents of self-regulation: A developmental perspective. *Developmental Psychology, 18,* 199–214.

Landry, S. H., & Smith, K. E. (in press). Early social and cognitive precursors and parental support for self-regulation and executive function: Relations from early childhood into adolescence. In B. Sokol, U. Müller, J.I.M. Carpendale, A. Young, & G. Iarocci (Eds.), *Self- and social-regulation: Exploring the relations between social interaction, social cognition, and the development of executive functions.* Oxford: Oxford University Press.

Lehto, J. E., Juujarvi, P., Kooistra, L., & Pulkkinen, L. (2003). Dimensions of executive functioning: Evidence from children. *British Journal of Developmental Psychology, 21,* 59–80.

Lewis, C., Carpendale, J. I. M., Towse, J., & Maridaki-Kassotaki, K. (in press). Epistemic flow and the social making of minds. In B. Sokol, U. Müller, J.I.M. Carpendale, A. Young, & G. Iarocc (Eds.), *Self- and social-regulation: Exploring the relations between social interaction, social cognition, and the development of executive functions.* Oxford, England: Oxford University Press.

Lewis, C., Solis-Trapala, I., Shimmon, K., & Diggle, P. (2009). *Test order effects in batteries of executive function in preschool children.* Manuscript in preparation.

Luria, A. R. (1961). *The role of speech in the regulation of normal and abnormal behavior.* Oxford: Pergamon.
Luria, A. R. (1981). *Language and cognition.* Chichester, England: Wiley.
Mead, G. H. (1910). What objects must psychology presuppose? *Journal of Philosophy, Psychology and Scientific Methods, 7,* 174–180.
Miller, S. A., Shelton, J., & Flavell, J. H. (1970). A test of Luria's hypotheses concerning the development of self-regulation. *Child Development, 41,* 651–665.
Mischel, W., & Baker, N. (1975) Cognitive transformations of reward objects through instructions. *Journal of Personality and Social Psychology, 31,* 254–261.
Miyake, A., Friedman, N. P., Emerson, M. J., Witzki, A. H., Howerter, A., & Wager, T. D. (2000). The unity and diversity of executive functions and their contributions to complex "frontal lobe" tasks: A latent variable analysis. *Cognitive Psychology, 41,* 49–100.
Moriguchi, Y., Lee, K., & Itakura, S. (2007). Social transmission of disinhibition in young children. *Developmental Science, 10,* 481–491.
Munakata, Y., & Yerys, B. E. (2001). All together now: When dissociations between knowledge and action disappear. *Psychological Science, 12,* 335–337.
Noble, K. G., McCandliss, B. D., & Farah, M. J. (2007). Socioeconomic gradients predict individual differences in neurocognitive abilities. *Developmental Science, 10,* 464–480.
Norman, D. A., & Shallice, T. (1980). *Attention to action: Willed and automatic control of behavior.* University of California at San Diego, CHIP Report 99.
Patterson, C. J., & Mischel, W. (1976). Effects of temptation-inhibiting and task-facilitating plans on self-control. *Journal of Personality and Social Psychology, 33,* 209–217.
Rabbitt, P. (1997). Introduction: Methodologies and models in the study of executive function. In P. Rabbitt (Ed.), *Methodology of frontal and executive function.* Hove, England: Psychology Press.
Ritchie, F. K., & Toner, I. J. (1984). Direct labeling, tester expectancy and delay maintenance behavior in Scottish preschool children. *International Journal of Behavioral Development, 7,* 333–341.
Rothbart, M., & Derryberry, D. (1981). Development of individual differences in temperament. In M. Lamb, & A. Brown (Eds.), *Advances in Developmental Psychology,* Vol. 1. Hillsdale: NJ: Erlbaum.
Russell, J., Mauthner, N., Sharpe, S., & Tidswell, T. (1991). The windows task as a measure of strategic deception in preschoolers and autistic subjects. *British Journal of Developmental Psychology, 9,* 331–349.
Sabbagh, M., Xu, F., Carlson, S. M., Moses, L. J., & Lee, K. (2006). The development of executive functioning and theory of mind: A comparison of Chinese and U.S. preschoolers. *Psychological Science, 17,* 74–81.
Shimmon, K. (2005). *The development of executive control in young children and its relationship with mental state understanding: A longitudinal study.* Ph.D. thesis, Lancaster University, England.
Smith, R. (1992). *Inhibition: History and meaning in the sciences of mind and brain.* Berkeley and Los Angeles: University of California Press.
Sokol, B. W., & Müller, U. (Eds.). (2007). The development of self-regulation: Toward the integration of cognition and emotion. (Special Issue.) *Cognitive Development, 22,* 401–567.
Subbotsky, E. V. (1976). *Psychology of partnership relations in preschoolers.* Moscow: Moscow University Press (in Russian).
Tardif, T., So, C. W-C., & Kaciroti, N. (2007). Language and false belief: Evidence for general, not specific effects in Cantonese-speaking preschoolers. *Developmental Psychology, 43,* 318–340.
Toner, I. J., Moore, L. P., & Emmons, B. A. (1980). Effect of being labelled on subsequent self-control in children. *Child Development, 51,* 618–621.
Toner, I. J., & Smith, R. A., (1977). Age and overt verbalisation in delay-maintenance behavior in children. *Journal of Experimental Child Psychology, 24,* 123–128.

Towse, J., Lewis, C., & Knowles, M. (2007). When knowledge is not enough: The phenomenon of goal neglect in preschool children. *Journal of Experimental Child Psychology, 96*, 320–332.

Vygotsky, L. S. (1978). *Mind in society: The development of higher psychological processes.* Cambridge, MA: Harvard University Press.

Zelazo, P. D., & Jacques, S. (1996). Children's rule use: Representation, reflection and cognitive control. *Annals of Child Development, 12,* 119–176.

Zelazo, P. D., & Müller, U. (2002). Executive function in typical and atypical development. In U. Goswami (Ed.), *Blackwell handbook of childhood cognitive development* (pp. 445–469). Oxford: Blackwell.

Zelazo, P. D., Müller, U., Frye, D., & Marcovitch, S. (2003). The development of executive function in early childhood. *Monographs of the Society for Research in Child Development, 68* (serial no. 274).

CHARLIE LEWIS, professor of family and developmental psychology at Lancaster University, conducts research on the family, especially the role of the father, and young children's understanding of mental states.

JEREMY I. M. CARPENDALE, professor of developmental psychology at Simon Fraser University, conducts research on social cognitive and moral development.

Bibok, M. B., Carpendale, J. I. M., & Müller, U. (2009). Parental scaffolding and the development of executive function. In C. Lewis & J. I. M. Carpendale (Eds.), Social interaction and the development of executive function. *New Directions in Child and Adolescent Development, 123*, 17–34.

2

Parental Scaffolding and the Development of Executive Function

Maximilian B. Bibok, Jeremy I. M. Carpendale, Ulrich Müller

Abstract

Research has demonstrated that differential parental scaffolding utterances influence children's development of executive function. Traditional conceptualizations of scaffolding, though, have difficulty in explaining how such differential effects influence children's cognitive development; they do not account for the timing of parental utterances with respect to children's currently occurring activities. We present a study examining the relationship between the timing of different parental scaffolding utterances and children's attention-switching EF abilities. There was a strong relation between the timing of elaborative parental utterances and attention switching. We discuss the implications of the findings for the conceptualization of the scaffolding process. © Wiley Periodicals, Inc.

Note: This research was supported by a Social Sciences and Humanities Research Council of Canada grant to the second and third authors.

In this chapter, we discuss the links between parental scaffolding and development of executive functioning (EF). First, we briefly introduce the concept of scaffolding as it is predominantly presented in the literature. Next, we review empirical research on the relation between scaffolding and cognitive development. In this context, we highlight the important role played by parental utterances. Afterwards, limitations in the traditional conceptualization of scaffolding are discussed—specifically, those pertaining to an explanation of why differential parental utterances have the effect they do on children's cognitive development. As an alternative framework by which to conceptualize the developmental impact of parental scaffolding utterances more accurately, an evolutionary epistemological account of scaffolding is presented and elaborated in this respect. Next, we detail a study examining the relationship between the timing of differential types of parental scaffolding utterances in the context of children's puzzle-solving activities, and those children's attention-switching EF abilities. Last, we discuss the implications of the findings for the conceptualization of the scaffolding process.

Traditional Conceptualization of Scaffolding

Broadly defined, scaffolding is the process by which tutors help plan and organize the activity of children so that they can *execute* a task that is beyond their current level of ability. Originally coined by Wood, Bruner, and Ross (1976), the concept of scaffolding was proposed as a model to account for how certain types of social interaction facilitate children's development. According to Wood and colleagues, the scaffolding process consists of six key subprocesses by which tutors facilitate children's cognitive and emotional development: (1) *recruitment* ("[Tutors] enlist [children's] interest in and adherence to the requirements of the task"; p. 98); (2) *direction maintenance* (tutors ensure that children's problem-solving activities are directed toward achieving particular outcomes that contribute to completion of the task); (3) *frustration control* (tutors manage and regulate children's negative emotional reactions to difficulties in solving the task in order to maintain their commitment to finishing the task); (4) *reduction in degree of freedom* ("[Tutors simplify] the task by reducing the number of constituent acts required to reach solution"; p. 98); (5) *marking critical features* (tutors make salient to children features or aspects of the task that are important or relevant for its completion); and (6) *demonstration* (tutors model "idealized" solutions to task requirements so that they may be imitated by children during completion of the task; p. 98). Through the incremental learning afforded children by the emotional and cognitively supportive social context of scaffolding, children eventually develop the skills necessary to solve tasks independently.

Scaffolding is therefore a process that simultaneously aims to regulate both children's motivation (recruitment, frustration control) and cognition (reduction in degree of freedom, marking critical features, demonstration). It is central to the scaffolding process that tutors should accommodate their support to match the current developmental level of the children they are assisting. Tutors must strike a balance between working with children at their current level of competency and at the same time challenging them. This requires that tutors not only respond contingently to children's ongoing activity but also expand on that activity and direct it in more challenging directions.

Directive and Elaborative Parental Scaffolding Utterances and Executive Function

Conceptually, the scaffolding process parallels executive function in terms of the cognitive and functional resources it affords children. In both situations an executive (either cognitive functions in the case of EF or a tutor in the case of scaffolding) helps children organize and plan their goal-directed activities. That is, in both situations children have access to meta-level cognitive resources that assist them in regulating their behavior. Tutors therefore perform many of the functional roles associated with EF on children's behalf. Consequently, parents and caregivers facilitate development of children's EF by setting a context in which children can gradually master those functions for themselves (see Landry, Smith, and Swank in this volume). For this reason, measures of parent-child scaffolding are expected to be predictive of children's EF.

A number of studies have investigated the relation between scaffolding and children's development of EF. Landry, Miller-Loncar, Smith, and Swank (2002) investigated the impact that parental verbal scaffolding of three-year-olds had on their later executive functioning at six years of age. Results showed that verbal scaffolding by parents was predictive of children's increased verbal ability at age four. In turn, this enhanced verbal ability was predictive of greater EF ability at six years of age. In a similar study, Smith, Landry, and Swank (2000) found that maternal scaffolding of children at three was predictive of greater verbal and nonverbal skills at six, even after controlling for SES and frequency of maternal stimulation (total scaffolding and nonscaffolding utterances). To account for these findings, Landry and colleagues (2002) suggested that through scaffolding parents give their children advanced language models by which to represent problems and their potential solutions. Parents who employed such elaborative, conceptually rich utterances were also observed to verbally guide their children's activities. This was in contrast to parents who relied instead on more directive and less conceptually informative utterances. Broadly viewed, the results of the study by Landry and colleagues suggest that instructive parental utterances can be classified into two broad categories: directive and elaborative. Of the two, elaborative utterances are predictive of greater EF development in children (Smith, Landry, & Swank, 2000).

A shortcoming of these studies is that they did not explicitly measure directive utterances as a category of parental utterances. Hess and McDevitt (1984) did code for such an utterance type. In a longitudinal study, Hess and McDevitt examined the relationship between maternal disciplinary and teaching techniques and children's developmental outcomes at four, five, six, and 12 years of age. Maternal utterances were categorized as either "direct commands" or "generative verbalizations" (p. 2020). Direct commands were defined as "unmoderated imperatives that call for either a verbal or nonverbal response" (p. 2021). Generative verbalizations were defined as maternal utterances, questions, comments, commands, and requests that called for children to generate a response of their own. They found that even after controlling for maternal verbal ability, SES, and mother's marital status, mothers' use of direct commands with their four-year-old children was negatively correlated with children's verbal ability at four years of age, and school readiness at five and six. Conversely, they found that maternal use of generative verbalizations was positively correlated with child outcomes. To refine their findings, Hess and McDevitt tested the possibility that mothers may intervene more directly to assist a struggling child. Neither of the correlations between direct command use and (1) child task inattention ($r = .08$, $p > .05$) or (2) number of correct task-specific responses ($r = .12$, $p > .05$) were significant. Hess and McDevitt interpreted these correlations as suggesting that the direction of effect between maternal direct command use and children's task-related difficulties could not be accounted for by child characteristics. These correlations can therefore be taken as suggestive of a causal relationship between maternal direct command use and negative child outcomes.

Consistent with the findings of Hess and McDevitt, Landry, Smith, Swank, and Miller-Loncar (2000) have also reported a negative relationship between maternal use of direct commands and children's later outcomes. Landry and colleagues studied the relationship between mothers' use of directive and maintaining behaviors with their children at two and three and a half, and those children's later social and cognitive abilities at four and a half (see Landry, Smith, and Swank in this volume for a discussion of the relationship between children's preschool skills and later social problem-solving outcomes). Maintaining behaviors were defined as either verbal or nonverbal behaviors that offered children choices (questions, suggestions, or comments) directly relevant to their current or immediately prior activities. Directive behaviors were defined as utterances giving children less opportunity for choice, instead emphasizing expected activities or behaviors. Results showed that although maternal directiveness may have a positive influence on development during toddlerhood, by three and a half years of age directiveness was predictive of lower developmental outcomes at four and a half. In contrast, the opposite relation was found for maternal use of maintaining behaviors at both two and three and a half. Landry and colleagues concluded that for scaffolding utterances to consistently assist children across development, directiveness of parental utterances must correspondingly decrease with children's increasing developmental competencies.

Taken together, the aforementioned studies suggest that (1) children's verbal ability is related to their cognitive performance; (2) children's verbal ability, in turn, is related to the verbal richness of parental utterances; (3) parental instructive utterances can be functionally categorized as either elaborative (verbally and conceptually rich) or directive in nature; (4) elaborative utterances are predictive of positive cognitive developmental outcomes in children; (5) conversely, directive utterances are predictive of negative cognitive developmental outcomes in children; (6) the negative impact of directive utterances cannot be completely accounted for by parental verbal ability or SES status (although see Hughes and Ensor in this volume for a discussion of contextual factors that influence parent-child scaffolding interactions); and (7) use of directive utterances cannot be solely attributable to child characteristics.

Parental Responsiveness and Executive Function

The preceding studies have empirically demonstrated an impact of parental scaffolding utterance type on the cognitive development of children. However, what remains to be determined is the relative developmental impact of those utterances, given their contingent occurrence in response to children's ongoing activities. For instance, the previously discussed study by Landry and colleagues (2000) incorporates such contingent responding in the definition of maternal maintaining behaviors, in that such behaviors are "related to the activity or object in which children were *currently* visually and/or physically engaged *just prior* to the mother's request" (p. 362, italics added). By either incorporating contingent responding in the definition of parental utterance types or failing to measure it separately from the frequency of utterance types, the relative developmental contribution of contingent responding with different utterance types cannot be determined. As such, whether or not the relative developmental impact of differential utterance types varies as a function of when they temporally occur in relation to the children's activities still needs to be addressed. As Landry and colleagues (2001, p. 387) point out, "In spite of the theoretical and clinical significance of the timing of responsive parenting, study designs often do not allow for its direct examination."

Parental responsiveness has been used as an indicator of such contingencies in a study by Landry and colleagues (2001) that examined the impact of maternal responsiveness on children's cognitive and social development over a developmental course spanning 6 to 48 months of age. Results showed that the frequency of responsive verbal and nonverbal behaviors mothers directed toward their children was positively predictive of positive developmental outcomes. Similarly, Kochanska, Murray, and Harlan (2000) found that maternal responsiveness ("promptness, engagement, sensitivity, acceptance, cooperation, availability, following child lead, adjusting stimulation to child state"; p. 225) measured at 22 months of age accounted for 6% of the variance in children's EF at both 22 and 33 months of age.

Limitations of the Traditional Conceptualization of Scaffolding

Although these studies demonstrate that maternal responsiveness per se is predictive of children's cognitive outcomes, they did not specifically measure the cognitive activity of children at the time of the maternal response. Without such knowledge, the findings of these studies cannot address potential models of how such responsiveness facilitates children's development. Both the scaffolding subprocesses originally proposed by Wood and colleagues and the directive and elaborative parental utterance types previously discussed are descriptions of the activities tutors perform while assisting children in solving a task. In the absence of a model of cognitive development, specific explication of how such subprocesses or utterance types facilitate cognitive development remains ill-defined (Bickhard, 1992; Renninger, Ray, Luft, & Newton, 2005). Instructive parental utterance types and the scaffolding process of Wood and colleagues both describe how scaffolding is done, but not why it comes to be done that way.

Evolutionary Epistemological Scaffolding

An alternative approach that can be employed in understanding the process of scaffolding follows from an evolutionary epistemological framework. Bickhard (1992), employing an evolutionary epistemological framework, has proposed that scaffolding should be viewed as the constructivist activity of a child in response to an epistemologically uncharted problem space. According to evolutionary epistemology, knowledge must be constructed by agents through their interaction with the world; knowledge cannot be internalized from a source outside the agent's own activity, such as the environment (Bickhard, 1992; Campbell & Bickhard, 1986). Agents are not epistemologically free to construct arbitrary knowledge but must operate within the constraints imposed by the world. These constraints, known as selection pressures, implicitly channel or guide the activity of agents. Stated more formally, selection pressures are implicit background conditions that must be satisfied before an activity can even be defined as a solution to a problem. If the constraints for a given problem are too far beyond an agent's level of ability, the agent will be unable to generate a solution to the problem, because any potential activity tried by the agent will be rendered inadequate by the constraints. In such situations, by reducing or muting the number of constraints (selection pressures) with which an agent must contend, a tutor can reduce the problem space so that the agent is able to construct a partial understanding of the original problem with whatever resources the agent has at its disposal. There are two ways of muting selection pressures: (1) reducing them by directly blocking them (for example, reducing task complexity, as in decreasing the size of the problem space) or (2) furnishing resources that satisfy them (external learning aids, marking critical feature, increasing the region of the problem space epistemologically transversable by the agent; cf. Wood, Bruner, & Ross, 1976). As this process in which tutors adaptively attenuate selection pressures on the agent's behalf continues, the agent slowly constructs, and accumulates, partial understandings of the original problem. Finally, a point will be reached were the agent will be in possession of enough cognitive resources (partial understandings) to solve the original problem by himself or herself.

Evolutionary Epistemological Scaffolding and Directive and Elaborative Parental Utterances

When viewed from an evolutionary epistemological perspective, it becomes possible to interpret the functional role of elaborative and directive utterances in terms of selection pressures. Directive utterances, by explicitly telling a child what to do, reduce the complexity of the task that the child must contend with. That is, directives decrease the size of the problem space defining a given task by directly blocking selection pressures the child encounters. Elaborative utterances, in contrast, furnish the child with external and auxiliary resources that increase the size of the problem space the child can epistemologically transverse.

Given such a definition of directive and elaborative utterances in terms of their effect on epistemic selection pressures, their effect on cognitive and EF development can be considered. Although directives may mute selection pressures to permit partial constructions, if they are too strong (simplify the task too much) there will be little necessity for the child to develop cognitively, because no new constructions are required to solve the task. This would correspondingly explain their negative effect on cognitive development; they delay the child's development, relative to peers, which appears as a negative outcome at later assessment. For example, Landry and colleagues (2000) found that directiveness might help development during the toddler years, but that this relation did not hold after toddlerhood. Rather, a shift from directing to maintaining behaviors (elaborative) by parents had to occur in parallel with their children's cognitive growth if such behaviors were to continue to support their children's development. Moreover, Landry and colleagues have suggested that directive utterances may require children to first abandon their present activity, and then orient elsewhere. By interfering with their attentional focus, directive utterances may be more cognitively demanding on children than maintaining behaviors. Elaborative utterances, in contrast, are "about" children's presently occurring activity. Consequently, elaborative utterances do not require that children disengage from their current activity before they can cognitively profit from such parental utterances.

In contrast to directive utterances, elaborative utterances, by augmenting cognitive resources, allow children to engage in novel partial constructions, yet do not permit them to rely solely on previous constructions. With respect to EF, elaborative utterances can be viewed as an auxiliary source of EF available to children. Elaborative utterances fulfil many of the roles attributed to EF: planning (requiring a capacity to disengage from the problem and reflect on it), attention switching (disengaging from a prior rule or stimulus), and inhibiting (disengaging from a prepotent response). By providing children with an auxiliary form of EF, elaborative utterances enable them to undertake partial constructions that will eventually result in construction of comparable EF capacities. For this reason, elaborative utterances would be expected to be predictive of cognitive development.

From an evolutionary epistemological framework, the influence of parental responsiveness is explainable in terms of the current cognitive activity of the child. If the child were undergoing a cognitive process of construction, utterances would be predicted to be most beneficial directly at those times when such construction is actively taking place. In contrast, utterances that do not occur during or immediately after the child's problem-solving activities may be more difficult for the child to associate with his or her prior activity. That is, such utterances would no longer serve as resources to help satisfy the selection pressures that were impinging on the child during the constructivist process.

Contingent Elaborative Utterances and Executive Function

The purpose of the present study was to investigate the relationship between elaborative and directive parental utterances contingent upon children's immediate cognitive activity and measures of children's cognitive EF. The study used a ring puzzle task (Carpendale, 1999) that "consisted of four concentric rings that were cut into equally sized pieces, grouped around a middle circle, and surrounded by a solid frame" (p. 136). The frame and all pieces were the same color. Puzzle pieces differed in their curvature, depending on which ring they were members of. Because they differed in curvature, incorrectly placed puzzle pieces produced a gap between themselves and neighboring pieces.

In a prior study with this ring puzzle, Schmid-Schönbein (1990) observed that children who spoke to themselves during completion of the task demonstrated increased understanding of the curvature principle in comparison to children who did not. Consistent with this observation, Carpendale (1999) found a similar result when children were asked certain forms of questions as they completed the task. Children who were asked to elaborate on their activities ("What are you doing now?," p. 136) demonstrated better performance on the task than children who were asked instead to pass judgment on their activities ("Does that piece fit?," p. 136). The findings of these two studies are consistent with those of the previously reviewed studies demonstrating a relationship between both children's verbal abilities and tutors' use of elaborative utterances, and children's cognitive performance. Together, the findings of Schmid-Schönbein and Carpendale suggest that the ring puzzle supplies a productive context in which to investigate the relationship between tutors' instructional utterances and children's cognitive performance.

We hypothesized that elaborative and directive parental utterances temporally contingent on children's ongoing cognitive puzzle-solving activity would be predictive of children's attention-switching EF. Although puzzle solving involves both cognitive and emotional factors, only children's activities that pertained to the cognitive aspects of the puzzle (for example, manipulation of puzzle pieces) were examined. Correspondingly, only children's attention-switching EF was examined. Of the various executive functions, attention switching would appear as the executive function most likely to be manifest during completion of the ring puzzle. If contingent parental utterances derive their effect on development by being relevant to children's cognitive activity at the time of their occurrence, then the measure of cognitive EF assessed needs to be as relevant to the children's puzzle-solving activities as possible. Attention-switching EF would manifest itself in children's ability to flexibly adjust their puzzle-solving behaviors in response to the errors they encounter in the course of solving the puzzle. That is, attention-switching EF would be expected to be inversely related to children's tendency to perseverate in unsuccessful puzzle-solving activities. Reciprocally, attention-switching EF would be expected to be directly related to children's ability to successfully complete the puzzle.

With respect to parental scaffolding of the ring puzzle, parental utterances serve to guide children's puzzle-solving activities. If children's puzzle-solving activities are in error, the only way children can viably continue to solve the puzzle is if they change their activity. By commenting on their children's activities in a temporally contingent manner (that is, during or after an erroneous activity), parents facilitate their children in either examining their own activity or switching to a new activity. That is, contingent parental utterances assist children in not perseverating in erroneous activities. Parental utterances can help children detect an erroneous puzzle-solving activity, or help them determine why a successful activity was productive (that is, why a successful activity was not in error). Parents therefore serve as an auxiliary and exogenous form of attention-switching EF for their children. Of the two other executive functions, inhibition and working memory, it is unclear what benefit parents could give their children by commenting on their activity so as to serve the roles of these executive functions. For example, inhibition may stop error perseveration, but will not assist children in switching to a more productive activity. Thus, with respect to children's own puzzle-solving activities and contingent parental utterances, the executive function of attention switching would appear to be the most pertinent to solving the task. Therefore, in the context of scaffolding of the ring puzzle, parental utterances temporally contingent on children's puzzle-solving activities are most likely to be related to children's attention-switching EF.

Because the same constructivist principles of either reducing or buttressing against selection pressures are thought to underlie other scaffolding relationships, the quality of the parent-child scaffolding relationship in the context of the ring puzzle task is likely to be representative of previous scaffolding relationships. The developmental influence of these previous scaffolding relationships, in turn, is likely to be reflected in children's attention-switching EF. Therefore, patterns of social interaction involving contingent parental elaboration and direction, observed during completion of the ring puzzle, are hypothesized to be predictive of children's attention-switching EF.

Participants, Procedure, and Results

To investigate this hypothesis, 36 parent-child dyads (33 mothers, three fathers; 21 male children and 15 female, 20 to 29 months, $M = 24.97$ months, $SD = 2.65$) participated in a study on the role of scaffolding in development of executive function. Participants were from the Greater Vancouver Region of Canada. Children were first assessed on a battery of attention-switching EF tasks. The shape stroop task (Carlson, Mandell, & Williams, 2004; Kochanska, Murray, & Harlan, 2000) measured children's ability to switch attention to the less salient of two perceptual features. The delayed alternation task (spatial reversal task; Landry, Miller-Loncar, Smith, & Swank, 2002) measured children's ability to alternate flexibly between differing search strategies to locate a hidden object among two possible spatial search locations. The reverse categorization task (Carlson, Mandell, & Williams, 2004) measured children's ability to switch between opposing rules for categorizing colored objects. Parents completed a demographic questionnaire and measures pertaining to their children's verbal ability (MacArthur Short Form; see Fenson, Pethick, Renda, Cox, Dale, & Reznick, 2000) and Internal States Language Questionnaire (ISLQ; Bretherton & Beeghly, 1982). Parents and their children were then videotaped as they completed the ring puzzle. Parents were instructed to help their children solve the puzzle, as they would do so at home. The puzzle took approximately eight minutes to complete.

Video footage of the ring puzzle task was time-coded for children's puzzle-solving activities and parental utterance type in order to create contingency scores of parental scaffolding. Children's puzzle-solving activities were assigned to three behavioral codes: (1) curvature (incorrectly placing a puzzle piece into a given space on the puzzle board), (2) backwards (placing a puzzle piece the wrong way around into the puzzle), and (3) correct (correctly placing a puzzle piece into the puzzle board). Task-relevant parental utterances were assigned to a pair of behavioral codes: (1) directive (utterances by the parent that command, direct, or state the *future* course of action the child should take next) and (2) elaborative (utterances by the parent that either elaborate on or evaluate the child's *presently* occurring course of action). Nonrelevant task utterances were not coded (cf. Freund, 1990). Both current context and preceding child utterances were used to disambiguate the assignment of behavioral codes to parental utterances.

Contingency scores of specific patterns of parental responsiveness were created by submitting these two measures to a lag-one sequential analysis (Bakeman & Gottman, 1986): the determination of the statistical probability that a given child's puzzle-solving activity type will be immediately overlapped or followed in time by a given parental utterance type. Contingency scores were computed using Yule's Q statistic. By crossing the three types of children's cognitive puzzle-solving activity code with the two types of parental utterance, two sets of contingency scores of interest were generated: directive and elaborative. Each set contained three contingency scores. For example, the elaborative contingency score set consisted of the transitions curvature → elaborative, backwards → elaborative, and correct → elaborative.

The choice to use a lag-one sequential analysis for construction of the contingency scores, and the direction of the interaction (transitions from child activity to parent response, rather than the opposite) was based on consideration of theoretical models of scaffolding (Bickhard, 1992; Wood, Bruner, & Ross, 1976). In these models it is the role of the tutor to decide how a task is to be decomposed. That is, the tutor's role has meaning and efficacy only if it is contingent on the child's current ability. Consequently, it is the child's activity that drives the scaffolding processes, with the tutor unable to accelerate the process beyond the constructivist capability of the child. In the context of the ring puzzle, because the task is novel to both parents and children, parents likely will be unable to rely on foreknowledge of their children's difficulties. This greatly reduces parents' anticipatory scaffolding of their children. Scaffolding of the task must instead be done online during actual completion of the task. Being unable to anticipate beforehand their children's difficulties, parents have to offer scaffolding support contingent on, and in response to, the ongoing activity of their children. It is for this reason that a lag-one sequential analysis of the specified direction was chosen.

To test the hypothesis of the present study, a data analytic approach was taken: a hierarchical regression was used to first control for variance in attention-switching EF attributable to (1) children's age, gender, and verbal ability (see Hughes and Ensor in this volume on the role of separating children's verbal abilities from their EF abilities), (2) parental education level, (3) frequency of child puzzle-solving activity types, and (4) frequency of parental utterance types. Contingency scores for the specific patterns of parental responsiveness were entered as sets in the next two steps in the regression. Directive contingency scores were entered first, followed by elaborative contingency scores. The change statistics (F-ratio test) were examined to determine the amount of variance by which each step increased the ability of the regression model to predict attention-switching EF, over and above that attributable to the prior steps, which collectively constituted restricted specifications of the model.

Initial examination of the full model revealed suppression (Conger, 1974; Velicer, 1968) between the directive and elaborative contingency scores involving children's correct puzzle piece placement and the other variables in the model. To protect against the possibility of spurious results owing to enhancement of the contingency scores via suppressor effects, these two contingency scores were dropped from the model. Consequently, each set of contingency scores consisted only of its respective curvature and backward contingency scores.

As predicted, elaborative contingency scores, when included in the fully specified model, were predictive of children's attention-switching EF ($\Delta F(2,18) = 4.230$, $\Delta R^2 = 0.122$, $p = 0.031$), whereas directive contingency scores were not, ($\Delta F(2,20) = 0.096$, $\Delta R^2 = 0.004$, $p = 0.909$). Moreover, the regression steps in which the simple frequencies of parental directive and elaborative utterances were entered into the model were not found to be significant (see Table 2.1).

Consistency with Prior Research

The purpose of this study was to determine if directive and elaborative utterances by parents, contingent on children's immediately occurring cognitive puzzle-solving activities, were predictive of those children's attention-switching EF. Results of the present study found that contingent elaborative responses, but not contingent directive responses, were predictive of children's attention-switching EF when included in the full model. This finding is largely consistent with previous studies that found elaborative, but not directive, utterances predictive of children's cognitive development (Hess & McDevitt, 1984; Landry et al., 2002; Smith, Landry, & Swank, 2000). Similarly, this finding is consistent with prior studies that found maternal responsiveness to be predictive of positive developmental outcomes (Kochanska, Murray, & Harlan, 2000; Landry et al., 2001). Particularly, the finding that elaborative contingency scores, but not directive contingency scores, were a significant predictor of EF is consistent with the finding by Landry and colleagues (2000) that for parental scaffolding to be predictive of children's cognitive development a shift from parental use of directive to elaborative utterances must occur over time.

Timing of Elaborative Utterances: Implications for Understanding the Scaffolding Process

The results demonstrate that the instructional value of elaborative scaffolding utterances does not lie solely in their content, but also in the timing of their delivery. Nonetheless, because directive contingency scores were not significant, instructional content clearly plays a role. If the mere timing of parental utterances was of instructional value, then directive contingency scores should also have been found to be significant. Rather, only elab-

Table 2.1. Summary of Hierarchical Regression Analysis for Variables Predicting 24-Month Attention-Switching EF Composite Scores (Final Model).

Variable	B	SE B	β	ΔR²
Step 1				0.090
Age	0.12	0.11	0.18	
Gender	0.77	0.56	0.23	
Step 2				0.038
Primary caregiver education				
College	0.45	0.93	0.09	
University degree	−0.59	0.64	−0.16	
Step 3				0.116*
MacArthur Short Form	−0.16	0.01	0.35*	
Step 4				0.086
MacArthur-Word Combination				
Sometimes	−2.28	1.32	−0.60	
Often	−2.52	1.33	−0.70	
Step 5				0.005
ISLQ	−0.01	0.03	−0.14	
Step 6				0.278**
Curvature	0.09	0.04	0.43*	
Backwards	−0.10	0.05	−0.33	
Correct	0.05	0.04	0.24	
Step 7				0.002
Directive	−0.02	0.05	−0.07	
Step 8				0.000
Elaborative	0.00	0.07	0.01	
Step 9				0.004
Curvature → directive	−0.20	0.47	−0.09	
Backwards → directive	0.04	0.43	0.01	
Step 10				0.122*
Curvature → elaborative	0.90	0.38	0.45*	
Backwards → elaborative	0.34	0.35	0.17	

Note: *$p < .05$; **$p < .01$.

orative contingency scores were found to be significant. Instead, part of what makes elaborative utterances instructional is their contingent delivery with respect to children's immediately occurring activities. If the value of elaborative scaffolding utterances was purely in their instructional content, then the regression step in which the frequency of elaborative utterances was entered into the model should have been found to be significant (see Table 2.1). What the statistical significance of the elaborative contingency scores broadly suggests is that for instructive utterances to have any effect at all on children's development they must first be contingent to the children's activities.

The results demonstrate a structural and temporal relationship between instructive utterances and children's cognitive activities. This finding is consistent with what would be predicted from an evolutionary epistemological account of scaffolding. That is, contingent utterances are expected to be most beneficial when they are relative to children's current cognitive activities. Moreover, the direction of the elaborative contingency scores used in this study were from child to parent transitions. This fact lends support to the notion that scaffolding is a process that is led by the child, with tutors adjusting and accommodating to the child's current level of performance. Specifically, it was the children's level of performance (that is, puzzle placement errors) that determined when parental elaborative utterances would be most predictive of children's attention-switching EF (see Table 2.1, step 10, curvature → elaborative regression coefficient).

What the findings of this study globally suggest, therefore, is that both scaffolding and cognitive development are inherently active processes. Knowledge cannot be imposed on individuals by the social environment. Rather, it is the agent's constructivist activities that make the environment intelligible. For example, simply exposing children to elaborative utterances does not guarantee that children will developmentally benefit from such utterances. Rather, such utterances must temporally occur in relation to children's activities such that children are able to construct the meaning of the utterances by relating them to their own activities. Thus scaffolding utterances are defined by how children cognitively use such utterances, and not by the purposes for which the tutor intended them. That is, the meaning of instructive utterances does not come from outside the children's own activity. Tutors can therefore facilitate children's development by timing their utterances so that they feed into the children's constructivist activities. Tutors cannot, however, circumvent the children's constructivist activity, nor externally or environmentally cause the children to develop.

Interactive Aspects of Scaffolding: Implications for Understanding Cognitive Development

With respect to the process of scaffolding, and cognitive development generally, the findings of this study have a number of implications. First, unlike the descriptive account of scaffolding proposed by Wood and colleagues, this study attempted to explicate the process of scaffolding as it unfolded in real-time social interaction. The findings of this study suggest that both scaffolding and cognition exploit the structural and temporal dimensions inherent in social and physical interaction (children's physical puzzle-solving activities that parents socially comment on, and children in turn understanding by associating with their current puzzle-solving activities). Scaffolding and cognition are as a result tightly coupled with the social and physical environments. That is, cognition is not a phenomenon that occurs asynchronously in relation to the social environment; it unfolds and takes place in real time with respect to the social environment. The sequential or temporal aspect of interaction, therefore, is of cognitive importance with respect to how individuals function in the world. This suggests that cognition may be inherently interactive and temporal in nature (Bickhard & Terveen, 1995) rather than representational. That is, representations, as symbols, are temporally invariant; the information they convey (what they symbolize or stand for) does not change with the passage of time. In contrast, interactions, as ongoing processes, are inherently temporal; the information they afford cognition is inherent in the organization of events over time and the timing of those events to one another; when an event occurred is as informative as the event that occurred. The finding that even after controlling for children's verbal ability elaborative contingency scores were predictive of children's attention-switching EF is suggestive of this view. For example, Landry and colleagues have proposed that scaffolding utterances support children's development by providing them with advanced language models by which to represent problems. If this were the only developmental role of elaborative utterances, then contingent elaborative utterances could have potentially turned out to be nonsignificant. Instead, the findings suggest that although language ability may play a role in the development of EF (see Table 2.1), the effect of contingent elaborative utterances on cognitive development is not completely mediated by language development. Moreover, because the language measures employed by this and other studies consisted of vocabulary measures, these measures of verbal ability may reflect children's representational abilities, rather than their ability to interactively use the temporal aspects of language (for example, turn taking) successfully in everyday contexts. It may be that as contingency scores reflect a real-time and interactive aspect of social interaction they capture those aspects of cognition that are interactive rather than representational in nature.

Limitations and Future Research Directions

A limitation of the study is that the findings are not generalizable to scaffolding situations outside the age group investigated (24 months). Cognition of toddlers is predominantly limited to their immediate surroundings and activities (Piaget, 1937/1954); that is, toddlers have restricted representational capabilities. Consequently, the cognitive activity of toddlers is directly manifest in their physical activities. Their physical activities can thus serve as an indicator variable or proxy for their cognitive activities. For parental utterances to contribute to toddlers' development, those utterances must co-occur with those toddlers' physical activities. The result of this scenario is that temporal contingencies (the measure of association of one event following another in time) can serve as an indicator or proxy variable for what actually are scaffolding contingencies of meaning (the association of meaningful utterances co-occurring in relation to cognitive activities of understanding). That is, the study successfully used temporal contingencies as a stand in for what might be called semantic or epistemic contingencies. With development, children become capable of representing and using language to refer to past and future activities. This means that children's cognitive activities need no longer map directly onto their physical activities as before. Thus, with the growth of children's ability to represent time, temporal and semantic contingencies begin to disassociate. Future research could address the empirical question of whether or not scaffolding contingencies, particularly their temporal dimension, remain consistent across development.

Another limitation of the study is that the inverse direction of contingency, with children's activities contingent on parental utterances, was not examined (Freund, 1990). Such contingencies, in conjunction with mother-to-child response contingencies, may create recursive patterns of interaction, which themselves may or may not predict children's EF. Furthermore, without controlling for child-to-mother response contingencies, the possibility that children may solicit parental support cannot be investigated (Freund, 1990). Such an effect would represent a form of self-scaffolding (Bickhard, 1992) or self-regulation (Freund, 1990) and so would be likely to have a direct relation to children's EF (see Landry, Smith, and Swank in this volume on the importance of initiating social interaction for development of EF and self-regulation).

To mitigate the limitations outlined, dynamic systems approaches to modeling social interaction could be used that would address the problems of recursion and child-to-mother response contingencies discussed. What is noteworthy in the present study is that the ability of elaborative contingency scores to predict attention-switching EF is quite strong considering the number of covariates that preceded its entry into the fully specified model, and the limited quantity of interaction sampled from each dyad. This suggests that microanalytic techniques that explore interaction in depth are capable of explaining the effect of social interaction on cognitive development with greater precision than other research methodologies. Together, microgenetic analytic techniques, such as sequential analysis, combined with longitudinal assessment to determine direction of causation would offer a new approach to the study of the relationship between social interaction and EF development (cf. Hendriks-Jansen, 1996).

Conclusion

The present study demonstrates that for children 24 months of age, scaffolding achieves its effects through timely presentation of elaborative parental utterances contingent on children's current cognitive activities. Implications of this finding are that the effects of social interaction on children's development cannot be reduced to the individual contributions of the participants. Rather, it is the interactive coupling between children and their caregivers that facilitates children's cognitive development. Early on in children's development, caregivers are primarily responsible for establishing and maintaining this interactive coupling. By following their children's lead, caregivers are able to offer their children elaborative utterance that are directly contingent on the children's cognitive activities. Children are able to cognitively profit from these elaborative utterances because they can easily associate such utterances with their immediate activities. With respect to development of executive function, parental elaborative utterances encourage children to reflect on their own activities. In this way, elaborative parental utterances serve as an auxiliary form of executive function that children can use to regulate their behavior. Continuous practice of such externally supported cognitive reflection allows children to eventually master and engage in such executive functioning on their own.

References

Bakeman R., & Gottman, J. M. (1986). *Observing interaction: An introduction to sequential analysis.* New York: Cambridge University Press.

Bickhard, M. H. (1992). Scaffolding and self-scaffolding: Central aspects of development. In L. T. Winegar & J. Valsiner (Eds.), *Children's development within social context: Vol. 1. Metatheory and theory* (pp. 33–52). Mahwah, NJ: Erlbaum.

Bickhard, M. H., & Terveen, L. (1995). *Foundational issues in artificial intelligence and cognitive science: Impasse and solution.* Amsterdam, Netherlands: Elsevier Science.

Bretherton, I., & Beeghly, M. (1982). Talking about internal states: The acquisition of an explicit theory of mind. *Developmental Psychology, 18,* 906–921.

Campbell, R. L., & Bickhard, M. H. (1986). *Knowing levels and developmental stages.* Basel, Switzerland: Karger.

Carlson, S., Mandell, D., & Williams, L. (2004). Executive function and theory of mind. *Developmental Psychology, 40,* 1105–1122.

Carpendale, J. I. M. (1999). Constructivism, communication, and cooperation: Implications of Michael Chapman's "epistemic triangle." In I. E. Sigel (Ed.), *Development of mental representation: Theories and applications* (pp. 129–146). Mahwah, NJ: Erlbaum.

Conger, A. J. (1974). A revised definition for suppressor variables: A guide to their identification and interpretation. *Educational and Psychological Measurement, 34,* 35–46.

Fenson, L., Pethick, S., Renda, C., Cox, J. L., Dale, P. S., & Reznick, J. S. (2000). Short-form versions of the MacArthur Communicative Development Inventories. *Applied Psycholinguistics, 21,* 95–116.

Freund, L. S. (1990). Maternal regulation of children's problem-solving behavior and its impact on children's performance. *Child Development, 61,* 113–126.

Hendriks-Jansen, H. (1996). *Catching ourselves in the act: Situated activity, interactive emergence, evolution, and human thought.* Cambridge, MA: MIT Press.

Hess R. D., & McDevitt, T. M. (1984). Some cognitive consequences of maternal intervention techniques: A longitudinal study. *Child Development, 55,* 2017–2030.

Kochanska, G., Murray, K. T., & Harlan, E. T. (2000). Effortful control in early childhood: Continuity and change, antecedents, and implications for social development. *Developmental Psychology, 36*(2), 220–232.

Landry, S. H., Miller-Loncar, C. L., Smith, K. E., & Swank, P. R. (2002). The role of early parenting in children's development of executive processes. *Developmental Neuropsychology, 21*(1), 15–41.

Landry, S. H., Smith, K. E., Swank, P. R., Assel, M. A., & Vellet, S. (2001). Does early responsive parenting have a special importance for children's development or is consistency across early childhood necessary? *Developmental Psychology, 37*(3), 387–403.

Landry, S. H., Smith, K. E., Swank, P. R., & Miller-Loncar, C. L. (2000). Early maternal and child influences on children's later independent cognitive and social functioning. *Child Development, 71*(2), 358–375.

Piaget, J. (1954). *The construction of reality in the child.* (M. Cook, Trans.). New York: Basic Books. (Original work published 1937)

Renninger, K. A., Ray, L. S., Luft, I., & Newton, E .L. (2005). Coding online content-informed scaffolding of mathematical thinking. *New Ideas in Psychology, 23,* 152–165.

Schmid-Schönbein, C. (1990, June). *Explicating some aspects of the process of reflective reconstruction.* Paper presented at the meeting of the Jean Piaget Society, Philadelphia.

Smith, K. E., Landry, S. H., & Swank, P. R. (2000). Does the content of mothers' verbal stimulation explain differences in children's development of verbal and nonverbal cognitive skills? *Journal of School Psychology, 38*(1), 27–49.

Velicer, W. F. (1968). Suppressor variables and the semipartial correlation coefficient. *Educational and Psychological Measurement, 38,* 953–958.

Wood, D., Bruner, J. S., & Ross, G. (1976). The role of tutoring in problem solving. *Journal of Child Psychology and Psychiatry, 17,* 89–100.

MAXIMILIAN B. BIBOK *is a doctoral student at Simon Fraser University, Burnaby, B.C., Canada.*

JEREMY I. M. CARPENDALE *is a professor of psychology at Simon Fraser University.*

ULRICH MÜLLER *is an associate professor of psychology at the University of Victoria, Victoria, B.C., Canada.*

Hughes, C. H., & Ensor, R. A. (2009). How do families help or hinder the emergence of early executive function? In C. Lewis & J. I. M. Carpendale (Eds.), Social interaction and the development of executive function. *New Directions in Child and Adolescent Development, 123,* 35–50.

3

How Do Families Help or Hinder the Emergence of Early Executive Function?

Claire H. Hughes, Rosie A. Ensor

Abstract

This chapter describes longitudinal findings from a socially diverse sample of 125 British children seen at ages two and four. Four models of social influence on executive function are tested, using multiple measures of family life as well as comprehensive assessments of children's executive functions. Our results confirm the importance of maternal scaffolding for young children's executive functions, but they also suggest positive effects of observational learning and adverse effects of disorganized and unpredictable family life; however, no support was found for an association between executive function and general positive characteristics of family interactions. © Wiley Periodicals, Inc.

Executive function (EF) is an umbrella term that encompasses the set of higher-order processes (such as inhibitory control, working memory, attentional flexibility) that govern goal-directed action and adaptive responses to novel, complex, or ambiguous situations (Hughes, Graham, & Grayson, 2005). Relations between social interactions and EF are, in research terms, largely *terra incognita*. Addressing this gap, this study examined two questions in particular. Compared with other neurocognitive functions, language and EF show protracted postnatal development and so are particularly susceptible to environmental influences (Noble, Norman, & Farah, 2005); our first question therefore concerned whether the associations between SES and EF/language reflect common or distinct underpinning mechanisms. Second, previous studies of social influences on early EF have focused on the role of maternal scaffolding (e.g., Bibok, Carpendale, and Müller in this volume). However, multiple processes mediate relations between SES and other cognitive domains, suggesting that scaffolding may be but one part of the jigsaw. To explore this possibility, we considered scaffolding alongside a range of other family factors (both positive and negative, direct and indirect) that are relevant to children's cognitive and social outcomes.

Research on EF Is Dominated by Biological Models

Several lines of evidence support an emphasis on biological influences on EF. For example, lesions to the prefrontal cortex (the core neural base for EF) are associated with decline in EF among older adults (Burke & Barnes, 2006) and individuals with head injury (Satish, Streufert, & Eslinger, 2006). Conversely, myelination of the prefrontal cortex is associated with age-related improvements in children's EF (Golden, 1981). Likewise, impairments in EF are widespread among childhood clinical disorders, and most pronounced among children with attention deficit hyperactivity disorder (ADHD) or autism (Pennington & Ozonoff, 1996), disorders that show substantial genetic influence (Kuntsi et al., 2004; Ronald et al., 2006).

However, none of these findings preclude social interactions from contributing to either developmental change or individual differences in EF. Current cognitive models of EF (e.g., Duncan, 2001) highlight the fluidity of relations between the prefrontal cortex and EF performance. Specifically, neurons within the prefrontal cortex show rapid adaptation to changing task demands (Freedman, Riesenhuber, Poggio, & Miller, 2001), making it difficult to map between behavioral and neuronal functions. This fluidity is also seen in a brain-imaging study of bilingual children, which demonstrated a culture- and language-specific activation of certain brain regions, specifically the inferior frontal gyrus and the temporo-parietal junction (Kobayashi, Glover, & Temple, 2007).

Evidence for Social Influences on EF

At least three types of evidence point to an association between social interactions and EF. First, although twin studies of cognitive impairments in older adults demonstrate that dementia is powerfully influenced by genes, such studies also highlight the importance of social influences on the age of onset and rapidity of cognitive decline (Gatz, 2007). Second, genetic factors often show substantial interactions with environmental influences, such that genetic vulnerability is expressed only among individuals exposed to environmental stressors, such as harsh parenting or family chaos (Asbury, Dunn, Pike, & Plomin, 2003; Asbury, Wachs, & Plomin, 2005). Third, intervention studies lend direct evidence for environmental effects on EF. For example, a recent randomized-control trial demonstrated that adults with autism showed improved performance on a battery of EF tasks after two years of supported employment (García-Villamisar & Hughes, 2007). Likewise, a meta-analytic review of cognitive remediation for individuals with schizophrenia revealed substantial improvements on EF tasks such as the Wisconsin Card Sort Test (Kurtz, Moberg, Gur, & Gur, 2001). Similar positive results were also reported in a recent training study involving typically developing preschoolers and a simplified version of the Wisconsin Card Sort (Kloo & Perner, 2003). The time is therefore ripe to investigate relations between early EF and social interactions.

Challenges for Research on Social Influences on EF

The paucity of existing research on social influences on EF also reflects the notorious difficulty of measuring environmental influences. One useful proxy is socioeconomic status (SES). Although genetic factors often co-vary with SES, environmental influences might be expected to be particularly strong for neurocognitive functions (such as language and EF) that show protracted postnatal development (Noble et al., 2005). In support of this view, Noble et al. (2005) reported that SES-related contrasts in cognitive performance were significantly stronger for language and EF than for other neurocognitive functions (e.g., vision, spatial cognition, memory). This finding raises the question of whether the associations between SES and EF/language reflect common or distinct underpinning mechanisms—a question that we hope to address in the present study.

As noted in several authoritative reviews (e.g., Bradley & Corwyn, 2002), individual differences in SES affect children's outcomes in a variety of ways, among them the quality of parent-child interactions, the general level of family chaos, and opportunities for observational learning. With regard to EF however, studies have focused heavily on one specific factor, namely the parental scaffolding of children's goal-directed activities. The term *scaffolding* is used to refer to how parental guidance enables children to achieve levels of problem solving they could not reach on their own. The emphasis on parental scaffolding reflects the theoretical dominance of Vygotskian perspectives on research into social influences on EF. Specifically, Luria's seminal work (1966) on the development of EF in childhood was heavily influenced by Vygotsky's accounts (e.g., 1962, 1978) of how interactions with a more competent social partner foster children's higher-order cognitive functions, and of how language plays a mediating role in this transfer from interpersonal to intrapersonal regulation.

Other chapters in this special volume (e.g., Bibok, Carpendale, and Müller) elaborate on the processes by which parents scaffold children's goal-directed activities. Our aim in this chapter is to address the challenge of offering a broader view, by considering scaffolding alongside a range of other family factors that are relevant to children's cognitive and social outcomes. If scaffolding is indeed the key to explaining why social interaction matters for children's EF, then our analyses should demonstrate that associations with other family factors become nonsignificant once scaffolding is included. If however, as we suspect, scaffolding is but one part of the jigsaw, then our analyses should reveal multiple independent predictive associations.

Four Competing Models of Social Influence on EF

Beyond scaffolding, what mechanisms might underpin associations between SES and children's developing EF? As noted earlier, mediators of SES-related contrasts in child outcomes are multiple and complex. Broadly speaking, a division can be made between mediators of SES effects on cognitive outcomes (which typically include cognitive stimulation, such as the literacy environment at home and at school) and mediators of SES effects on behavioral outcomes (which include parental warmth or negativity, disciplinary strategies, and general family climate). However, early individual differences in EF show consistent associations with both academic outcomes (McClelland, Cameron, Connor, Farris, Jewkes, & Morrison, 2007) and behavioral adjustment (Hughes & Ensor, in press; Valiente, Lemery-Chalfant, & Reiser, 2007). As a result it is possible that the full spectrum of environmental influences contribute to individual differences in EF.

The first model considered in this study was the *global positive model*, which emphasizes positive processes such as mother-child talk and calm response to a child's transgressions. A role for mother-child talk is suggested by studies demonstrating that language ability mediates the association between SES and EF (e.g., Noble, McCandliss, & Farah, 2007; Noble et al., 2005). Thus family factors that contribute to individual differences in language ability (e.g., quantity and complexity of mother-child talk, Hoff, 2003) may also underpin individual differences in EF. Supporting a role for calm parental response in promoting EF, recent findings (Valiente et al., 2007) show that calm and positive parental responses to children's negative emotions enhance children's "effortful control," a component of emotion-related regulation that is closely related to EF.

The second model was the *global negative model*, which emphasizes background negative factors such as disorganization and unpredictability in family life. Here it's worth noting that in the 2007 study by Valiente et al. family chaos was negatively associated with calm parental responses. In addition, Atzaba-Poria and Pike (2008) have reported that adverse family characteristics, such as fathers' favoritism toward individual children, are predicted by the level of family chaos.

The third model was the *imitation model*, which highlights the importance of children's observational learning. As noted by Dunn (1993), from a remarkably early age children are extremely acute observers of family life, paying close attention to injustices such as parents' differential treatment of siblings. This point can be applied to young children's observational skills more generally; most parents will be able to recall many episodes in which their children have mimicked their actions with uncanny accuracy. This attention to detail is likely to favor children's rapid mastery of complex action plans: though simple mimicry of adults' planful behavior does not, in and of itself, constitute executive control, acquiring a repertoire of "goal-directed" acts is likely to promote development of EF.

The fourth model was the *scaffolding model*, which highlights individual differences in parental support and guidance during children's goal-directed activities. Here, a key point to note is that scaffolding reflects parents' *deliberate* efforts to support children's goal-direct activity. In contrast, the other models described here indicate pathways by which parents can *unknowingly* influence children's EF performance. Demonstrating that family influences on EF extend beyond specific effects of parental scaffolding therefore has both theoretical and practical significance; we return to this point in our discussion. We turn now to describing the study: the sample, the various measures of social interaction, and our assessments of the young children's EF skills.

Maternal and Family Characteristics of the Study Sample

The sample of 125 children (78 boys and 47 girls) was recruited from toddler groups in and around Cambridge, UK; reflecting the characteristics of the local population, all but five of the children came from Caucasian families. However, compared with the relatively homogeneous and prosperous family backgrounds of samples typically studied by developmental researchers, the current sample includes a large proportion of children from disadvantaged families (i.e., low-income, lone-parent, or teen-parent families). For the analyses reported in this chapter, we adopted two widely used markers of SES: maternal education and head-of-household occupational status. The distribution of maternal education was as follows: 10%

had no educational qualifications, 26% had only basic (age 16) educational qualifications, 36% had age 18 educational qualifications, and 28% had a degree. Likewise, there was also a wide distribution of occupational status for family head of household: 23% were in unskilled labor, 28% were in skilled labor, 11% were in administrative or technical occupations, and 38% were in managerial or professional occupations.

The social diversity of the sample is a clear strength of the study because there is evidence to suggest that SES effects are strongest at the bottom end of the scale (Scarr, 2000). One reason for this is that certain environmental measures (e.g., ratings of family chaos) may show significant variance only if low SES families (who are most at risk of exposure to multiple stressors) are included within research studies. Additional strengths of the study included the variety of measures employed to index family life (see below), the comprehensive battery of EF tasks (see subsequent section), and the study's two-year longitudinal design. By testing the children at age two and again at age four, we were able to control for initial individual differences in EF. Taking the temporal stability of individual differences in EF into account is important; this minimizes the confounding effects of genetic factors (Kovas, Haworth, Dale, & Plomin, 2007).

Multiple Measures of Family Life

The study included diverse measures of social interaction. These included detailed video-based coding of mother-child interactions in multiple settings, maternal self-report questionnaires, and indices of maternal planning and self-monitoring obtained from a novel experimental task. For each of the four models tested, we selected particular measures as independent variables, using the findings from the existing literature to justify our choice. For reasons of space, these measures are summarized in Table 3.1, with one exception: a newly developed experimental measure of maternal planning (the "Six Things" task), which we describe below.

The Six Things task was designed to engage mothers having few educational qualifications and was adapted from a paper-and-pen task in the Test of Everyday Attention for Children (Heaton et al., 2002). We introduced the task by explaining we thought it likely that many children picked up the organizational skills they needed at school by watching their mothers doing chores at home. To mimic this scenario, we asked mothers to complete six simple tasks in six minutes. The tasks were two analogue wrapping tasks (wrapping a snack and wrapping a drink carton), two analogue sorting tasks (sorting two types of candy by color), and two analogue happy-face tasks (making a happy face using either stickers or drawing pins). The mothers were given a stopwatch for timekeeping and told that the most important thing was to have a go at all six tasks, without doing any two analogue tasks consecutively.

Table 3.1. Study Measures.

Type	Measure	Source	Scaling Information	Descriptive Statistics
Global positive	Mean length of utterance (MLU)	Transcript	Unstructured family interaction around evening meal	Mean = 8 (SD = 2.6); range = 3–20 words
	Calm response to transgression	Mother questionnaire (Arnold, O'Leary, Wolff, & Acker, 1993)	10 seven-point items, e.g., "After there's been a problem with my child, things get back to normal quickly"	Mean = 31 (SD = 5.6); range = 15–42; Cronbach's alpha = .73
Global negative	Family chaos	Mother questionnaire (Coldwell, Pike, & Dunn, 2006; Matheny, Wachs, Ludwig, & Phillips, 1995)	6 five-point items, e.g., "It's a real zoo in our home"	Mean = 15 (SD = 4.2); range = 6–24; Cronbach's alpha = .67
	Inconsistent parenting	Mother questionnaire (Arnold et al., 1993)	10 seven-point items, e.g., "When I make a fair threat, I often don't carry it out"	Mean = 18 (SD = 6.6); range = 6–41; Cronbach's alpha = .72
Imitative learning	Experimental self-monitoring measure	Six Things task	No. of times task completed within 70 seconds	Mean = 3.3 (SD = 1.9); range = 0–6
	Experimental planning measure	Six Things task	E.g., preparing strips of sellotape in advance; tipping the candy onto a tray to facilitate sorting	Mean = 2.1 (SD = 1.7); range = 0–7
	Real-life planning measure	5-minute mother-child video of Tidy-up task (Gardner, Sonuga-Barke, & Sayal, 1999)	Frequencies of reasoning, bargaining, compromising, and imaginative suggestions	Mean = 2.5 (SD = 2.8); range = 0–17
Scaffolding	Positive control	10-minute mother-child video of structured play (Deater-Deckard, Pylas, & Petrill, 1997)	Global 0-to-6-point scale, based on frequency of open-ended questions, praise, or encouragement and elaboration	Mean = 3.7 (SD = 0.7); range = 0–6

Relations Between Family Measures, and Associations with SES

Two global positive measures, the parent's Mean Length of Utterance (MLU) and Calm Parenting, were constructed. They were unrelated to each other ($r = -.09$, ns), but each was significantly related to maternal education and head-of-household occupational status, our two markers of family SES (average $r = .25$, $p < .01$). The two global negative measures (family chaos and inconsistent parenting) were unrelated to each other ($r = -.07$) and unrelated to family SES (average $r = .07$). With regard to the imitative learning model, the two six-things measures (planning and self-monitoring) were significantly correlated ($r = .20$, $p < .05$); planning was also correlated with tidy-up strategies ($r = .18$, $p < .05$), whereas self-monitoring was not ($r = .02$, ns). That said, self-monitoring was significantly associated with our markers of family SES (average $r = .24$, $p < .01$); but neither experimental nor observational measure of maternal planning was related to SES (average $r = .04$, ns). Maternal scaffolding was also significantly associated with both markers of family SES (average $r = .22$, $p < .05$).

Measuring Verbal Ability and Executive Function in Young Children

Verbal Ability. Raw scores from the vocabulary and comprehension subtests from the British Abilities Scales (Elliott, Murray, & Pearson, 1983) were used to assess children's vocabulary and verbal comprehension at age two. Standard scoring procedures were applied and gave a possible range of 0 to 20 points for vocabulary and 0 to 27 for comprehension. The British Picture Vocabulary Scale (Dunn, 1997) was used to assess children's vocabulary at age four.

Executive Function (EF). In the past, tests of EF for children have generally been simplified versions of adult tasks. However, for very young children with limited language skills, this approach has only limited success. A more promising strategy is to adapt tasks that have been developed for animal studies. In our study we combined these two approaches and worked hard to ensure that the tasks built on young children's interests (cf. Hughes & Ensor, 2005). For example, the first task in the battery was Spin the Pots, a multilocation search task in which children had to find stickers hidden in six of eight attractive and visually distinct boxes on a Lazy Susan tray, which could be covered and spun between trials. This kind of foraging task is appealing to most young children and so served as a good icebreaker for the rest of the session. Performance was measured by the number of trials required to find all six stickers.

A second task was a variant of the Stroop task, in which children have to inhibit a prepotent response in order to execute a less familiar response. We presented this task as a topsy-turvy game, involving "mummy-sized" and "baby-sized" cups and spoons. On each of 12 trials in the baby Stroop task, the researcher showed the child a cup or spoon and the child was asked to say "Mummy" if presented with a baby-sized item or "Baby" if presented with a mummy-sized item. Performance was measured by the number of correct trials. A third task capitalized on young children's interest in winning treats. This Trucks task required children to learn a rule (point to one truck in each of two pairs) and then to learn the inverse rule. A criterion of five consecutively correct trials was used to index rule mastery, and performance was indexed by the number (0–2) of rules learned. A fourth Beads task was taken from the Stanford-Binet Intelligence Scales (Thorndike, Hagen, & Sattler, 1986). On each trial of this task, children are briefly shown one or two beads and asked to find the matching bead(s) from a picture of beads arranged by color (red, white, blue) and shape (sphere, cone, oblate spheroid); in a more advanced part of this task children are given the beads and a peg and asked on each trial to construct an array that matches a picture shown for just five seconds. Performance was measured by the number of correct trials. The final task presented at age two was the "detour-reaching box" (Hughes & Russell, 1993), a shiny metal box with a window through which children could reach to retrieve a marble placed on a platform. However, direct reaches through this window activated an infrared sensor, causing the marble to drop out of sight through a trapdoor. In the warm-up phase, children had to inhibit this reaching action and retrieve the marble using a knob and paddle (rather like pinball). In the test phase, the knob route was blocked by a padlock and children had to coordinate two actions: flicking a switch (to block the infrared sensor) and then reaching in to retrieve the marble. Success on each route was indexed by three consecutively correct trials. Performance was rated by the number of trials needed to succeed on the test phase.

At age four, children received the same first four tasks as at age two; the Detour-Reaching Box was replaced by the more complex Tower of London task (Shallice, 1982). The Tower of London task presents children with planning problems graded in difficulty. At the simplest (warm-up) level, children are given an array of three squashy balls on three pegs of unequal size (small, medium, and large) and shown a slightly different array, which they are asked to match by moving just one ball. This is followed by a set of three two-move problems, three three-move problems, and three four-move problems. For each problem, children received two points for a perfect solution (i.e., matching the goal arrangement in the specified minimum number of moves) and one point for an adequate solution (i.e., matching the goal arrangement by a less efficient set of moves); to ensure that children did not become discouraged they were given two attempts at each problem, but only scores on the first attempt were included in our analyses.

Correlations between scores on individual tasks ranged from .10 to .30 at age two (mean r = .18, p < .05) and from –.07 to .42 at age four (mean

$r = .16, p < .07$). The low mean between-task correlation at age four resulted from a ceiling effect on the Pots task (scores on this task at age four were unrelated to scores on all other tasks). The Pots task was therefore excluded from the aggregate age four EF measure, which was thus based on four tasks (Stroop, Beads, Trucks, Tower of London). The internal consistency of the EF index was modest at age two (alpha = .63) and good at age four (alpha = .78). The construction of a single aggregate was also supported by the results of principal component factor analyses (with varimax rotation for maximum clarity of factor solutions), which yielded one single factor at each time point, accounting for 39% and 47% of the total variance at ages two and four respectively. The factor loadings ranged from 0.57 to 0.67 at age two and from 0.59 to 0.77 at age four.

Results

As expected, individual differences in EF were very stable from ages two to four: the correlation between scores across these time points was .58, indicating that age two EF scores predicted just over a third of the variance in age four EF scores. Individual differences in EF were also closely associated with individual differences in verbal ability at each time point (average $r = .50$). Together, age two EF and concurrent verbal ability explained 48% of the variance in EF at age four. This substantial proportion of explained variance, coupled with reports that language mediates effects of SES on EF (Noble et al., 2005, 2007), made it quite likely that our measures of family life would not predict any further independent variance in age four EF.

With regard to our first question, concerning the specificity of family influences on EF versus verbal ability, it is worth noting that several family measures showed marginal or significant correlations with individual differences in age four EF, even with effects of age two EF and age four verbal ability controlled (see Figure 3.1). Several predictors were also related to individual differences in verbal ability at age four (see Figure 3.2). Interestingly however, the contrast in the strength of correlation between maternal scaffolding and age 4 EF versus verbal ability approached significance (1-tailed $z = 1.54, p = .06$), providing some support for the view that maternal scaffolding has a relatively specific effects on young children's EF performance. We turn now to our second question, concerning the extent to which family influences on EF extend beyond effects of maternal scaffolding. Logically, a specific effect of scaffolding on EF is compatible with the hypothesis that young children's EF performance is associated with a variety of aspects of family life. To investigate this proposal, we entered each of the measures at the second step of a regression analysis (with age four EF as the dependent variable and effects of initial EF and concurrent verbal ability controlled at the first step). Associations with maternal education, head-of-household occupational status, and mother-child talk measure were each attenuated, the association with

Figure 3.1. Correlations Between Age Four EF and Family Measures.

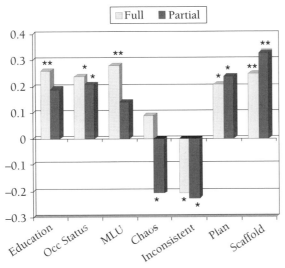

Note: Partial correlations controlling for effects of age two EF and age four verbal ability are shown in parentheses.

Figure 3.2. Correlations Between Age Four Verbal Ability and Family Measures.

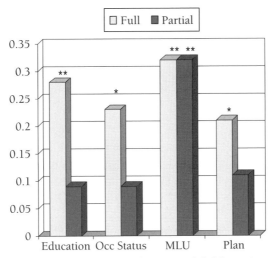

Note: Partial correlations controlling for effects of age two verbal ability and age four EF are shown in parentheses.

inconsistent parenting became marginal, but associations with the three other measures (maternal planning, maternal scaffolding and family chaos) remained significant, jointly accounting for an additional 14% of the variance in age four EF.

Discussion

The first question addressed by this study concerned the relative overlap or independence of social influences on EF and verbal ability. Here, the breadth of measures included in the present study was valuable. Specifically, our findings demonstrate that although certain aspects of children's social environments (such as the quality of mother-child talk) show overlapping associations with individual differences in EF and verbal ability, other aspects (such as maternal scaffolding) were more specifically associated with EF. These findings return us to a point raised at the start of this paper, namely the parallel and interacting effects of biological factors.

Specifically, two lessons from the recent findings of a large-scale twin study (Kovas et al., 2007) deserve mention. First, although genetic factors are typically general in their impact, environmental influences have much greater specificity. The independent associations among EF and scaffolding, maternal planning, family chaos, and inconsistent parenting are therefore less likely to show confounding effects of genetic factors than is the more general association between mother-child talk and EF/verbal ability. Second, whereas genetic factors are of primary importance in explaining stable individual differences, environmental factors are important for understanding change. This conclusion suggests that the longitudinal design of this study was crucial to its success in demonstrating associations between social influences and emerging EF. By controlling for individual differences in EF at age two, our analyses focused on variation in *change* in EF performance between the ages of two and four.

The second question addressed by this study concerned four models of social influence on early EF. The first, global positive, model was the only one that our findings did not support; once effects of age two EF and concurrent verbal ability were controlled, neither of the two general measures of positive family interactions (mother-child talk and calm parental responses to transgressions) was related to age four EF. In other words, as one might expect, general positive influences showed overlapping influences on EF and verbal ability and contributed to continuity rather than change in EF.

With regard to our second, general negative, model it is interesting that family chaos and inconsistent parenting were unrelated to our measures of socioeconomic background. Also of note is the finding that the association between family chaos and age four EF became evident only after effects of age two EF and concurrent verbal ability were controlled. Effectively then, family chaos appeared associated with (lack of) improvement in EF between the ages of two and four. Together with the marginally significant unique association with inconsistent parenting, this finding highlights the potential adverse effects of a disorganized and unpredictable family environment on young children's growing abilities to hold things in mind, plan and execute goal-directed acts, and suppress impulse-driven responses.

Our third, imitative learning, model received partial support from our study findings; children's EF scores at age four were associated with maternal planning on the six-things task but were unrelated to maternal strategies during the observed tidy-up sessions (even though these two measures were significantly correlated with each other). One possible explanation for this contrast is that, compared with the tidy-up task, the six-things task afforded a purer measure of maternal planning strategies. This is because the tidy-up task presents mothers with the dual challenge of achieving the goal (tidying up) and maintaining a harmonious interaction with the child. The six-things task is a new measure of maternal planning; the present findings support its construct validity and predictive utility. Further research is, however, needed to establish its reliability and replicate the findings presented here.

Finally, our study findings also supported the fourth, maternal scaffolding, model: individual differences in the extent to which mothers engaged in open-ended questions, praise, encouragement, or elaborations during a structured activity predicted individual differences in children's EF performance at age four. This predictive relationship remained significant even when age two EF scores, age four verbal ability, family background, and other social interaction measures were all taken into account.

Taken together, our findings suggest that multiple aspects of social interactions underpin individual differences in EF in young children. This conclusion highlights the importance of a broad approach that extends beyond the traditional focus on parental scaffolding. As noted earlier, one potentially important contrast between scaffolding and predictors such as maternal planning, family chaos, and inconsistent parenting hinges on the deliberate versus incidental nature of their influences on children's EF. That is, although scaffolding encompasses parents' deliberate efforts to support and guide children's goal-directed activity (via open-ended questions, elaborations, praise, and so on), the other measures reflect individual differences in children's incidental exposure to family environments that can help or hinder goal-directed thought and action.

Caveats and Conclusions

This study represents a first step in exploring the processes through which families both help and hinder young children's emerging executive functions. As such, the findings require replication. As illustrated by the contrasting associations between physical discipline and child problem behaviors in European versus African American families (Deater-Deckard & Dodge, 1997), the correlates of specific family processes are likely to be culturally specific. Further work is therefore needed to establish whether our findings can be extended beyond this white British sample. It would also be valuable for future work to extend the developmental scope of this study, to establish whether the reach of early social influences on EF extends across the transition to school. At this stage, however, the results of this study carry clear practical implications. In particular, our findings suggest that children's growing EF skills can be supported in a variety of ways: by caregivers' conscious efforts at supporting and guiding goal-directed activities; by providing children with opportunities to observe adults' own planning strategies; by clear, consistent parenting that enables children to predict the consequences of their actions; and by ensuring that family chaos does not thwart children's efforts at developing goal-directed thought and action.

References

Arnold, D., O'Leary, S., Wolff, L., & Acker, M. (1993). The parenting scale: A measure of dysfunctional parenting in discipline situations. *Psychological Assessment, 5,* 137–144.

Asbury, K., Dunn, J., Pike, A., & Plomin, R. (2003). Nonshared environmental influences on individual differences in early behavioral development: A monozygotic twin differences study. *Child Development, 74,* 933–943.

Asbury, K., Wachs, T., & Plomin, R. (2005). Environmental moderators of genetic influence on verbal and nonverbal abilities in early childhood. *Intelligence, 33,* 643–661.

Atzaba-Poria, N., & Pike, A. (2008). Correlates of parental differential treatment: Parental and contextual factors during middle childhood. *Child Development, 79,* 217–232.

Bradley, R., & Corwyn, R. (2002). Socioeconomic status and child development. *Annual Review of Psychology, 53,* 371–399.

Burke, S., & Barnes, C. (2006). Neural plasticity in the ageing brain. *Nature Reviews Neuroscience, 7,* 30–40.

Coldwell, J., Pike, A., & Dunn, J. (2006). Household chaos: Links with parenting and child behaviour. *Journal of Child Psychology and Psychiatry, 47,* 1116–1122.

Deater-Deckard, K., & Dodge, K. (1997). Externalizing behavior problems and discipline revisited: Nonlinear effects and variation by culture, context, and gender. *Psychological Inquiry, 8,* 161–175.

Deater-Deckard, K., Pylas, M., & Petrill, S. (1997). *Parent-Child Interactive System (PARCHISY).* London.

Duncan, J. (2001). An adaptive coding model of neural function in prefrontal cortex. *Nature Reviews Neuroscience, 2,* 820–829.

Dunn, J. (1993). *Young children's close relationships: Beyond attachment.* Newbury Park, CA: Sage.

Dunn, L. (1997). *British Picture Vocabulary Scale—Revised.* Windsor, England: NFER-Nelson.

Elliott, C., Murray, D., & Pearson, L. (1983). *British Abilities Scales.* Windsor, England: NFER-Nelson.

Freedman, D. J., Riesenhuber, M., Poggio, T., & Miller, E. K. (2001). Categorical representation of visual stimuli in the primate prefrontal cortex. *Science, 291,* 312–316.

García-Villamisar, D., & Hughes, C. (2007). Supported employment improves cognitive performance in adults with autism. *Journal of Intellectual Disability Research, 51,* 142–150.

Gardner, F., Sonuga-Barke, E., & Sayal, K. (1999). Parents anticipating misbehaviour: An observational study of strategies parents use to prevent conflict with behaviour problem children. *Journal of Child Psychology and Psychiatry, 40,* 1185–1196.

Gatz, M. (2007). Genetics, dementia, and the elderly. *Current Directions in Psychological Science, 16,* 123–127.

Golden, C. (1981). *Diagnosis and rehabilitation in clinical neuropsychology.* Springfield: Charles C. Thomas.

Heaton, S., et al. (2002). The Test of Everyday Attention for Children (TEA-Ch): Patterns of performance in children with ADHD and clinical controls. *Child Neuropsychology* (Neuropsychology, Development and Cognition: Section C), *7,* 251–264.

Hoff, E. (2003). The specificity of environmental influence: Socioeconomic status affects early vocabulary development via maternal speech. *Child Development, 74,* 1368–1378.

Hughes, C., & Ensor, R. (2005). Theory of mind and executive function in 2-year-olds: A family affair? *Developmental Neuropsychology, 28,* 645–668.

Hughes, C., & Ensor, R. (in press). Does executive function matter for preschoolers' problem behaviors? *Journal of Abnormal Child Psychology.*

Hughes, C., Graham, A., & Grayson, A. (2005). Executive function in childhood: Development and disorder. In J. Oates (Ed.), *Cognitive Development* (pp. 205–230). Milton Keynes: Open University Press.

Hughes, C., & Russell, J. (1993). Autistic children's difficulty with mental disengagement from an object: Its implications for theories of autism. *Developmental Psychology, 29,* 498–510.

Kloo, D., & Perner, J. (2003). Training transfer between card sorting and false belief understanding: Helping children apply conflicting descriptions. *Child Development, 74,* 1823–1839.

Kobayashi, C., Glover, G., & Temple, E. (2007). Cultural and linguistic effects on neural bases of "Theory of Mind" in American and Japanese children. *Brain Research, 1164,* 95–107.

Kovas, Y., Haworth, C., Dale, P., & Plomin, R. (2007). *The genetic and environmental origins of learning abilities and disabilities in the early school years* (Vol. 72). Boston: Blackwell.

Kuntsi, J., et al. (2004). Co-occurrence of ADHD and low IQ has genetic origins. *American Journal of Medicine Genet B Neuropsychiatry Genet, 124*(1), 41–47.

Kurtz, M., Moberg, P., Gur, R. C., & Gur, R. E. (2001). Approaches to cognitive remediation of neuropsychological deficits in schizophrenia: A review and meta-analysis. *Neuropsychology Review, 11,* 197–210.

Luria, A. R. (1966). *Higher cortical functions in man* (1st ed.). New York: Basic Books.

Matheny, A., Wachs, T., Ludwig, J., & Phillips, K. (1995). Bringing order out of chaos: Psychometric characteristics of the confusion, hubbub, and order scale. *Journal of Applied Developmental Psychology, 16,* 429–444.

McClelland, M., Cameron, C., Connor, C., Farris, C., Jewkes, A., & Morrison, F. (2007). Links between behavioral regulation and preschoolers' literacy, vocabulary, and math skills. *Developmental Psychology, 43,* 947–959.

Noble, K., McCandliss, B., & Farah, M. (2007). Socioeconomic gradients predict individual differences in neurocognitive abilities. *Developmental Science, 10,* 464–480.

Noble, K., Norman, M. F., & Farah, M. (2005). Neurocognitive correlates of socioeconomic status in kindergarten children. *Developmental Science, 8,* 74–87.

Pennington, B., & Ozonoff, S. (1996). Executive function and developmental psychopathology. *Journal of Child Psychology and Psychiatry, 37,* 51–87.

Ronald, A., et al. (2006). Genetic heterogeneity between the three components of the autism spectrum: A twin study. *Journal of the American Academy of Child & Adolescent Psychiatry, 45,* 691–699.

Satish, U., Streufert, S., & Eslinger, P. (2006). Measuring executive function deficits following head injury: An application of SMS simulation technology. *Psychological Record, 56,* 181–190.

Scarr, S. (2000). American childcare today. In A. Slater & D. Muir (Eds.), *Blackwell reader in developmental psychology.* Oxford: Blackwell.

Shallice, T. (1982). Specific impairments in planning. *Philosophical Transactions of the Royal Society of London, B298,* 199–209.

Thorndike, R. L., Hagen, E. P., & Sattler, J. M. (1986). *Stanford-Binet Intelligence Scales.* Chicago: Riverside.

Valiente, C., Lemery-Chalfant, K., & Reiser, M. (2007). Pathways to problem behaviors: Chaotic homes, parent and child effortful control, and parenting. *Social Development, 16,* 249–267.

Vygotsky, L. (1962). *Thought and Language.* Cambridge, MA: MIT Press.

Vygotsky, L. (1978). *Mind in society: The development of higher psychological processes.* Cambridge MA: Harvard University Press.

CLAIRE H. HUGHES is a reader in developmental psychology in the Department of Social and Developmental Psychology at the University of Cambridge, a research group leader at the university's Centre for Family Research, and a fellow of Newnham College, Cambridge, England.

ROSIE A. ENSOR is a postdoctoral fellow of the British Academy affiliated to the Centre for Family Research at the University of Cambridge and a postdoctoral teaching associate at Kings' College, England.

Landry, S. H., Smith, K. E., & Swank, P. R. (2009). New directions in evaluating social problem solving in childhood: Early precursors and links to adolescent social competence. In C. Lewis & J. I. M. Carpendale (Eds.), Social interaction and the development of executive function. *New Directions in Child and Adolescent Development, 123*, 51–68.

4

New Directions in Evaluating Social Problem Solving in Childhood: Early Precursors and Links to Adolescent Social Competence

Susan H. Landry, Karen E. Smith, Paul R. Swank

Abstract

A major objective of this chapter is to present a novel, ecologically sensitive social problem-solving task for school-aged children that captures the complexity of social and cognitive demands placed on children in naturalistic situations. Competence on this task correlates with a range of skills including executive functions, verbal reasoning, and attention. Children able to successfully carry out this task in middle school were more competent in early adolescence in collaborating in joint problem-solving tasks with peers and solving conflicts with parents. © Wiley Periodicals, Inc.

Note: This study was supported by NIH Grant HD25128. Address correspondence to Susan H. Landry, Children's Learning Institute, Dept. of Pediatrics, University of Texas-Houston Health Science Center, 7000 Fannin Ste. 2300, Houston, TX 77030 (phone: 713/500–3709; e-mail: susan.landry@uth.tmc.edu).

To more fully understand social competence in everyday settings, it appears necessary to capture integration of skills rather than measurement of individual skills. This requires development of measurement approaches that provide a score reflecting the child's ability to bring skills together flexibly to work with others. This chapter describes development of such a measure and supports its usefulness by linking children's competency during middle childhood to early precursor skills and later, more complex social challenges in adolescence.

By middle elementary school, children are expected to interact in social contexts without a high degree of structure and support from others. Social interactions at this age often become complex when demands are placed on children to consider others' points of view as well as their own and offer information based on the knowledge they possess. Children can show success with these demands if they are demonstrating, to some extent, the ability to perceive and respond to the goals of others as well as others' perceptions and beliefs (Tomasello, Kruger, & Ratner, 1993). Competency in shared interactions with others requires a range of cognitive, social, and verbal skills. From the social domain, children need to understand the behavior of others, including that they potentially have different perspectives, intentions, and knowledge (Astington & Jenkins, 1999; de Villiers & Pyers, 2002; Slomkowski & Dunn, 1996). For this to occur effectively, they need to perceive social cues and alter their strategies on the basis of the feedback received from a social partner. Cognitively, a child is required to attend (sustained attention, short-term memory) and use information to plan and reason how to organize behaviors to achieve problem solving with others (executive functioning). Flexible use of verbal skills may complement these more specific cognitive abilities. Integration of the many skills needed to function in more complex social situations is referred to in this chapter as *social problem solving*.

The ability to plan, sequence behaviors, and alter problem-solving strategies on the basis of feedback is often referred to as involving executive processing (Welsh & Pennington, 1988). Many theorists believe this is a critical set of behaviors for social competence (Lezak, 1982; Rourke & Fuerst, 1991) because they help the child organize the information from the environment and process it to effectively comprehend social experiences. Developmentalists also emphasize that social problem-solving requires behaviors such as goal directedness and planning and frequently describe it under the rubric of self-regulation (Eisenberg, Fabes, Guthrie, & Reiser, 2000). For children to function competently, given the complexity of social situations, they also require the ability to create new strategies for use in novel situations and self-monitor in order to inhibit behaviors that are not appropriate for the demands of the social context (Carlson & Moses, 2001; Hughes, 1998). Integration of these skills is occurring across childhood (Astington & Pelletier, 2005), but there is a protracted developmental course where these skills increase in complexity by entry into adolescence, are multidimensional, and can vary flexibly depending on the social context (Steinberg, Dahl, Keating, Kupfer, Masten, & Pine, 2006; Steinberg, 2005)

Although middle childhood is an important developmental period for integration of multiple skills to meet the complexity of social situations, the foundation for them has its roots in infancy. In infancy and early childhood, parental support allows the child to learn to regulate behavior with consistent responsiveness from the caregiver to guide this developmental course (Landry, Smith, & Swank, 2006). Gradually, the child begins to assume more control and can by early elementary school become more autonomous in carrying out the complex set of skills required for problem solving in social situations. Thus, to capture a child's competence in social problem solving, measurement procedures need to place demands on the child's self-regulatory, executive processing, and social engagement. Additional basic skills that are also involved in social problem solving are competent language, regulation of attention, and memory.

In this chapter we address three goals. The first is to describe an approach to measurement of social problem solving that captures the complexity of social and cognitive demands placed on children in naturalistic situations. As part of this goal, we evaluate the extent to which children's skills on this measure related to a broad range of abilities expected to be needed for competence in social problem solving. Because theorists hypothesize that competence in this area during middle childhood should establish a positive trajectory for social competence at later ages (Steinberg, 2005), our second goal is to determine if skill in the social problem-solving measure predicts competence in problem solving with peers and parents in early adolescents. Finally, we explore the early precursors to competence on this new measure, including the role of early social interactions, pretend play, and language.

These objectives are addressed with data from a longitudinal research program involving 360 children and their parents recruited from three large hospitals in infancy and followed through early adolescence. The sample included one group of infants born at very low birthweight ($n = 224$) and a second group of infants born at term ($n = 136$) that were demographically similar to those born preterm. Cumulative attrition from the original cohort to the 13-year age point was 27% and due mainly to relocation and loss of contact. No significant differences on the demographic variables were found for those who remained in the study versus those who did not.

Home visits were made to collect observed behaviors during the Monopoly and peer problem-solving tasks at eight years and to administer the cognitive and executive functioning tasks. At 13 years of age, children's interactions with peers in two problem-solving tasks were also observed during home visits. We describe relations between observational and standardized measures of the children's social and play skills at three years and six-year language skills with eight-year social problem-solving competence.

Goal 1: Measurement of Social Problem Solving

Current Approaches and Drawbacks
There are standardized ways to individually measure cognitive, social, language, and executive function skills. For example, social development is typically measured through parent and teacher rating scales (Achenbach & Rescorla, 2001), whereas cognitive and language skills are measured with standardized tests of intelligence and receptive and expressive language (Sattler, 2008). Additionally, numerous tests have been developed to specifically examine executive function skills such as the Tower of London (Shallice, 1982) and attention is often measured with computer-based tasks (Halperin, Sharma, Greenblatt, & Schwartz, 1991). However, approaches for capturing integration of these skills in ecologically sensitive ways are not well established, especially for school-aged children. The value of observing such behaviors in everyday situations with real-world demands has been noted by others (Isquith, Gioia, & Epsy, 2004) and is frequently used in research with young children (Landry, Chapieski, Richardson, Palmer, & Hall, 1990; Landry, Miller-Loncar, Smith, & Swank, 2002).

One reason ecologically sensitive measures are less often used is that reliance on observational methods can produce a number of observed variables. A dilemma with this approach is that the individual variables do not yield a single score that captures the integrated skills (or underlying construct) the approach was intended to measure. Important issues in developing scoring procedures are which dimensions to measure and specific scoring methods for quantifying the behaviors captured in a social problem-solving situation.

Traditional rating scales, such as those found in parent and teacher report questionnaires (Achenbach & Rescorla, 2001), use a summative approach where individual items designed to measure the underlying construct of interest are added together to produce an estimate of the individual's "true" score. The degree to which an individual item contributes to the total score is a function of its variance and correlation with other items. Items with greater variance and those that tend to correlate highest with the remaining items get more weight in the total; that is, they constitute a greater proportion of the total score variance. Thus, even though summative rating scales may do an adequate job of describing individuals at the center of the scale, they do not generate as much information at the extremes of the distribution.

A Novel Measurement Approach. Our first goal was to develop an ecologically sensitive measure of social problem solving that required the child to integrate a broad range of cognitive and social skills in order to solve problems with others. A related goal was to develop a scoring approach that permitted capturing competency in integration of these skills in a single score. Our intent was to place demands on the school-age child's ability to understand when a person needed information about the rules of a game and to supply the information needed to keep the game moving forward. In this task, the child is first led to believe that his social partner is naïve because she does not have knowledge about the rules of the game. The child is also led to believe that this partner has a desire to learn the game so that she can play with the child. Thus the task is conducted in a manner that would make "human sense" (Donaldson, 1978) to the child and therefore trigger a motivation for teaching the partner. Because playing board games is a naturally occurring activity in which children engage with others, we explored whether use of a board game (Monopoly, Jr.) in a shared activity task would capture an integration of the skills required in social problem solving.

A competency score from this task incorporated children's ability to take initiative, respond to cues, and alter strategies given feedback from a partner. Children were expected to be more competent in this activity if they maintained awareness that they had knowledge needed in order to play, were able to read the nonverbal signals of their adult partner, appreciated that their partner needed information when appearing confused or hesitant, and offered such information clearly and coherently. An effective way to capture integration of multiple skills is through Rasch scaling, which can estimate an underlying behavioral construct from observed behaviors. This approach differs from the summative approaches used with the traditional rating scales in a number of ways. First, it makes available an estimate of the observed behaviors that are linearly related to a single underlying construct. By defining a model in which an individual's behaviors are seen as a function of its value on the measurement construct, the construct is estimated. Because the observed value is a direct estimate of the construct, its reliability, or the degree to which the observed scores reflect the "true score," is the *consistency* of estimating the construct. Validity, or the degree to which the true scores on the test reflect the underlying construct, is the *accuracy* of estimating the construct. By using this approach, reliability and validity are more integrated because the observed data are related to the underlying construct rather than to the true score on the test. Second, given that this approach yields better variability in scores at the extremes of the distribution than traditional methods, it amounts to a more accurate assessment of each subject.

Task Administration. Administration of the Monopoly social problem-solving task involved two steps. First, a 20-minute teaching phase involved one examiner acting as a "teacher" to ensure that the 17 major rules needed to play were known by the child. Some rules had multiple parts, ranging from one to three, and this was incorporated into the scoring system. To assess rule understanding, the child was asked to describe each rule during play. At the end of this phase, the examiner stated the need to stop and do "paperwork" and asked the child to play the game with a second examiner. This second observer told the child she (the examiner) did not know how to play and needed the child to "teach the game."

For each of the 17 rules, the novice examiner did not make a move until a full rule explanation was furnished or the maximum of three queries by the examiner was given. The queries increased in the specificity of information regarding the rule in question; level 1 provided an open-ended prompt, level 2 oriented the child to an aspect of the rule, and level 3 offered all necessary information with a request for a yes-no reply (see Appendix for examples). For children who were unable to explain four basic rules necessary to start the game, the procedure was discontinued.

Coding of Observed Behaviors. For each of the 17 rules, three aspects of the child's provision of information were coded: (1) completeness of information (full, partial), (2) number of queries required (none, one, two, or three), and (3) answer to level 3 queries when required (agreed, denied). Interrater reliability was .86 to .96, established for each of the coded behaviors (Fleiss, 1986; Frick & Semmel, 1978). The scores for the three aspects of the child's behaviors over the rules for each child were used to obtain a single social problem score based on a Rasch modeling approach using the Winstep procedure (Linacre, 1991–2004). Children received a higher score if able to effectively provide information to the examiner about the rules.

Development of a Social Problem-Solving Score. The use of Rasch modeling is based on the assumption that there is an underlying unidimensional continuum of skills, or construct, and that the responses to the task items were a function of this underlying continuum (Andrich, 1988). For each rule, a score was assigned on the basis of developmental expectations that ordered children's responses in terms of use of full or partial explanations, number of queries, and agreement with level 3 queries. A child who required zero queries and gave a full verbal explanation would have the highest score, while a child who required three queries but then denied that the last query was accurate would have the lowest score. Children's responses across items were then subjected to a principal axes factor analyses; six factors were found that accounted for 100% of the common factor variance and 31% of the total variance. The factors were moderately correlated (.12 to .56, with a median correlation of .42). Then further Rasch scaling was done to derive a single social problem-solving score. Given these correlations, it was assumed that the task is relatively unidimensional. When averaged across subjects, the mean social problem-solving construct score was 0.73 ($SD = 0.66$), and the reliability was .78. The Rasch score is in logit units, which typically range from –5.0 to +5.0. In our sample, the Rasch score ranged from –1.61 to 4.44, with 90% in the –.31 to 1.77 range.

Interpretation of Social Problem-Solving Scores. Children who received higher scores were adept at playing the game and providing helpful information to the novice partner with fewer queries. However, even the highest-scoring children were not able to supply full explanations on the majority of items without some queries. Those children who had the lowest scores had considerable difficulty in sharing information independently without multiple queries that often required a level 3 cue (gave all of the information necessary to move play forward). Their difficulty seemed to stem, in part, from a lack of understanding of their role of teacher in relation to their social partner. Children with lower scores often appeared to be in parallel play with the naïve partner. Those children with scores closer to the mean were better able to understand that sharing information was required, offered basic information about the need to perform certain critical game functions (need for money, need to roll the dice) but struggled in supplying information logically and cohesively. For instance, these children might attempt to explain that buying property is required but not understand that their partner needed to also know that property was bought from the bank by the person landing on a particular piece of real estate. Thus their information was too sketchy to allow their social partner to play the game.

Association with Concurrent Cognitive Skills. To verify that the social problem-solving construct score was in fact measuring children's cognitive and language characteristics of the child as conceptualized, it was necessary to examine relations with a set of measures of these skills that were also collected on this sample of children. Cognitive skills included short-term memory, attention, executive functioning, and verbal reasoning. Evidence of the sensitivity of this task to individual differences in children's developmental status, including age and biological risk (preterm vs. term birth) status, also would be important to document.

Short-term memory was measured with two subtests from the Stanford-Binet Intelligence Scale, 4th Ed. (SB-4; Thorndike, Hagen, & Sattler, 1986), Bead Memory and Memory for Sentences. Verbal reasoning was measured by the SB-4 subtests Vocabulary, Comprehension, and Absurdities. The ability to sustain attention was measured by the Continuous Performance Task (CPT; Halperin et al., 1991) and the Tower of London (TOL; Shallice, 1982) was the measure of executive functioning. In this task, children are asked to remember a set of basic rules. Regulation of behavior is required because of the need to shift strategies according to examiner feedback. Difficulty on this measure can be related to children's inability to consistently follow the rules or perseveration on a strategy may occur rather than trying a new approach (Raizner, Song, & Levin, 2002).

As hypothesized, the Monopoly task appears to require a range of cognitive and language skills, as supported by significant relations between the social problem-solving score with specific skill areas that range from .28 to .42 (see Table 4.1). In general, children with higher social problem-solving scores showed higher memory skills, better attention, and more developed executive functioning. Significant relations were also found with the verbal reasoning scores from the Stanford-Binet Intelligence test. This demonstrated that children with better verbal reasoning skills had higher social problem-solving scores. We also found that older children and those with

Table 4.1. Concurrent Relations at Eight Years of the Monopoly Score with Individual Skill Scores and Child Characteristics.

	Monopoly Score
Cognitive	
Short-term memory (STM, SB-4)	.33***
Inattention (CPT)	−.34***
Total correct solutions (TOL)	.28***
Verbal	
Verbal reasoning (VR, SB-4)	.42***
Child characteristics	
Chronological age (CA)	.16*
Gestational age (GA)	.27***

Note: $* p < .05$; $** p < .01$; $*** p < .0001$.

lower biological risk were more likely to perform better than younger children and those born at greater biological risk.

Summary. The Monopoly task comprised three behaviors that were then considered together for development of a single competence score. A high score should represent a child who was able to attend to the novice partner's need for information about the rules of the game without lapsing in this role, and to clarify when the partner appeared hesitant or confused. This also required remembering the sequence of rules they had been taught and offering these rules in a logical and organized manner. Thus, higher-scoring children required few prompts and tended to provide more complete information at the time it was needed. Low competency was conceptualized to represent a child who knew how to play the game, as evidenced by the success had in playing the game during his or her own turn, but an inability to work effectively in sharing knowledge. Results of the Rasch modeling met many critical criteria required for such an approach, including good reliability of respondent scores and item consistency. The scores obtained through this approach were well within an acceptable range and permitted calculation of a single score, demonstrating that the three responses across the 17 items were a function of one underlying behavioral construct. We expected that the construct, which we refer to as social problem solving, would require a range of cognitive and language skills. Although the task was developed on the basis of this conceptualization, empirical evidence was needed to ensure that skill on this task was in fact related to this broad range of skills.

Given the relations found between the social problem-solving score and a range of cognitive measures, one question that arises is why a task is needed that captures some of the same skills. To date, there are limited approaches for capturing children's ability to integrate a broad range of skills necessary to understand effective social problem solving in everyday situations. Because children may appear to have average skills in many tasks when assessed independently, they can be observed to have more difficulty when placed in more demanding social situations where the skills have to be used together flexibly. The ability to use these skills together could be considered more than the additive effect of use of skills independently. The Rasch modeling approach achieved the ability to capture this multifaceted skill because one construct score was demonstrated that related to an array of cognitive and social abilities. Relations support the idea that the social problem score is related to, but not the same as, the individual cognitive and language skills.

Goal 2: Does Competency in Social Problem Solving in Middle Childhood Predict Early Adolescent Social Competence?

Problem Solving with Peers

Young adolescents have the challenge of making and maintaining friends with limited support from adults, and this requires a range of underlying competencies, among them the ability to negotiate, inhibit frustration, take into account others' ideas and perspectives, and act on multiple pieces of information in problem-solving situations with peers (e.g., Steinberg et al., 2006; Keller, Edelstein, Schmid, Fang, & Fang, 1998). The ability to function collaboratively with same-age peers in early adolescence is considered an important developmental goal (Steinberg, 2005). Skills required for working collaboratively with peers are expected to develop across middle childhood in social situations where the child must attend to the goals of a social task and maintain efforts to engage effectively with others. If this process is to be successful, these competencies need to be developing during middle childhood. Support for this hypothesis would come, in part, from relations between social problem-solving skills in middle childhood and social competence with peers in early adolescence.

To establish that the earlier social problem-solving Monopoly scores were sensitive to children's development of similar behavior at later ages, we examined relations between the Monopoly ability and peer competence factors at 13 years. Social engagement with peers was evaluated during two 15-minute sessions with the target child and two peers. Task instructions included the directive to the group to plan and implement play goals together. Interactive behaviors coded using a time sampling procedure included behaviors such as comments and cooperation with peer requests. Global ratings were used to capture behaviors that reflected more dispositional characteristics such as social engagement and frustration tolerance

Figure 4.1. Relations Between Eight-Year Social Problem-Solving Construct Skill Scores and 13-Year Joint Collaboration with Peers and Verbal Engagement with Parents During a Conflict Resolution Task.

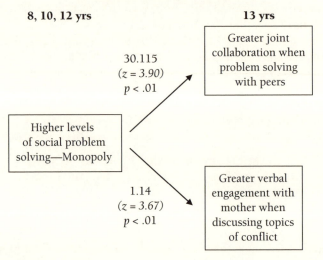

(Hebert-Myers, Guttentag, Swank, Smith, & Landry, 2006). Generalizability coefficients for the behaviors ranged from .83 to .99 (Frick & Semmel, 1978). Factor analyses revealed four factors: social connectedness, frustration tolerance and flexibility, compliance to requests, and noncompliance with requests.

Support for goal 2 was seen by the eight-year Monopoly score significantly predicting joint collaboration with peers at 13 years ($F(1, 392) = 4.58$; $p < .04$; Figure 4.1). Children with higher scores on the Monopoly task were more likely to be engaged and working effectively with peers. While the Monopoly task placed demands on children's ability to accommodate another person's lack of competency, it provided a high degree of structure including assurance that the child had an adequate knowledge base and probes to help guide their input to the partner. In contrast, the social problem-solving situation with peers in early adolescence was highly unstructured and novel, thus, placing a higher level of demand on the child to use a range of skills in order to be effective. Challenges to effective peer collaborations include remaining engaged with others in working on the task, understanding that peers may think about things differently and appreciating their knowledge base and perspective. This is more challenging than working with an adult as peers are less likely to accommodate and provide support for the young adolescent's social needs. Our results demonstrate that the child first learns to accomplish social problem-solving skills in a context with adults where some support is provided to help them organize their behavior in order that they can later carry this out more independently with peers.

Problem Solving with Parents. Another social milestone associated with adolescence is getting along with adults, including the ability to resolve conflicts. The most recent meta analysis of this literature supports the notion that the frequency and intensity of parent-child conflicts generally declines across adolescence (Laursen, Coy, & Collins, 1998). Studies document that parent-adolescent interactions increase in conflict (for example, bickering) from early to mid-adolescence (Kim, Conger, Lorenz, & Elder, 2001; McGue, Elkins, Walden, & Iacono, 2005) and that positive maternal affect declines over this period (Loeber, Drinkwater, Yin, Anderson, Schmidt, & Crawford, 2000). Across later adolescence, the parent-child relationship appears to reorganize such that the overall picture is a decline in conflict across the entire adolescent period (Loeber et al., 2000). Healthy relations with a parent would include the adolescent openly discussing and solving problems together as well as disclosure of information about activities and whereabouts. The adolescent who has developed a range of regulatory skills while entering into this developmental phase that includes even greater need for autonomy is more likely to be successful in differentiation from his or her parent(s). It is important to note, however, that the research in this area has focused primarily on Western cultures (Wenxin, Meiping, & Fuligni, 2006). Thus the extent to which these patterns generalize to other cultures is not understood. Similar to our objective in understanding the relation between earlier problem solving on the Monopoly task with peer interactions at 13 years, we expected similar relations between the Monopoly skills and resolving conflicts with parents.

At 13 years, measurement of conflict resolution skills was based on the protocol by Rueter and Conger (1998), where adolescents and their mothers complete a checklist to rate level of conflict for various topics (such as homework). The examiner determines the four most conflictual topics and asks the pair to resolve each of them by answering four questions. The interaction is videotaped and coded for maternal and adolescent behaviors. Multiple adolescent behaviors are coded using rating scales ranging from 1 (not at all characteristic) to 5 (very characteristic). Generalizability coefficients for the adolescent behaviors during this task all were > .80 (Frick & Semmel, 1978). Factor analyses of the coded behaviors revealed three positive factors and one negative, listening and enjoyment, positive verbal engagement, quantity and quality of solutions, and denial and disruptive processes. Again, we see support for the hypothesis that social problem-solving skills developing across middle childhood establish a foundation for using these skills in adolescence in more complex social contexts such as resolving conflict with an adult. For example, the Monopoly skills predicted positive verbal engagement in the conflict task (Figure 4.1). Strong relations were also found with quantity and quality of solutions.

Summary. Although the Monopoly task was not expected to place high emotional demands on the child, the conflict resolution task did involve heightened emotional tension. This task is consequently more complex because to be effective the adolescent must manage emotional reactions including the need to mask feelings when the other person initiates conflicting ideas. A foundation of more effective control of impulses and ability to take another's perspective, skills required in the Monopoly task, likely contributes to the adolescent's ability to be more reflective and manage emotions when discussing problem areas with a parent.

Goal 3: Early Childhood Precursors to Social Problem Solving in Middle Childhood

Role of Early Social Skills

Theories of socialization suggest that children first learn to regulate their behavior when interacting with caregivers and then generalize these skills to interactions with others (Feldman & Klein, 2003; Kochanska & Murray, 2000; Kuczynski & Kochanska, 1995). In the preschool period, this includes the ability to initiate conversation, use language to communicate needs, and successfully cooperate with requests made by caregivers (Landry, Smith, Swank, Assel, & Vellet, 2001). Thus one would expect that an important developmental precursor to competency in shared activities with others is the young child's social competence with caregivers. A child's ability to take the lead in social interactions with caregivers is also thought to contribute to an internal knowledge base that fosters competence in shared activities with a social partner other than the parent. Feldman and Klein (2003) note that support for this notion requires linking early social behavior with caregivers to later social competency with others. Such links have been shown in relation to impulse and behavioral control (Kochanska, 2002), but less frequently related to competencies in shared activities with others.

Role of Early Play Skills. We expected that another skill with roots in early childhood, important for the skills required in the Monopoly game task, was solitary pretend play (Bretherton, 1984; Piaget, 1962). Play has been described by developmental psychologists as being of great importance in promoting cognitive development and ultimately appears to lead children to development of skills necessary for more complex problem solving (Bruner, 1972; Piaget, 1962). Play during infancy typically involves single objects, but as children age problem solving during play becomes increasingly complex as they integrate multiple play materials and engage in pretend play (Fenson, Kagan, Kearsley, & Zelazo, 1976). When playing with objects, goal-directed behaviors are evident in children's selection of play materials and how they sequence their behavior to achieve goals. The act of role playing during pretend play may have important links to later competency in shared activities; role playing allows a child to begin to understand that the members of a scenario might have different needs and perspectives (Wolf, Rygh, & Altshuler, 1984).

Predictors of Middle School Social Competence. Early social communication skills with parents and pretend play were expected to have their influence on the skills required in the Monopoly task through influence on early school age language abilities measured at six years. Through early interactions with caregivers, children develop a knowledge of social relations, conversational rules in using language, and flexibility in using language to match the demands of a social context (such as pragmatics; Snow, 1999; Imbens-Bailey & Snow, 1997). School-aged language development may also be the conduit through which pretend play establishes a foundation for later competency in working effectively and sharing information with others. Through pretend play, children learn how to symbolically represent real-life situations and act out social scenarios. Being able to represent roles symbolically is considered a critical precursor for development of language, because children need to understand how to use words to represent real objects or life situations (McCune-Nicolich, 1981).

Measurement of Play and Language. We have previously described use of an independent goal-directed play task that involves observation of children's play with multiple toys presented sequentially (Landry, Smith, Swank, & Miller-Loncar, 2000). In this chapter, these observations included children's use of simple and pretend play. Simple pretend was coded when toys were used in a way that suggested an inanimate object had life (as with a character knocking on a door, or pushing a car down the road). Complex pretend play included animation that demonstrated the ability to sequence two or more play actions (for example, a figure walks up to a door and knocks; two characters each take a turn in a conversation). These two play scores were used for the pretend play construct. A standardized measure of language development, the Clinical Evaluation of Language Fundamentals—Preschool version (Wiig, Secord, & Semel, 1992), was used to measure receptive and expressive language skills at six years. For this sample, the mean standard score for receptive language was 93.11 ($SD = 14.10$) and for expressive language 88.89 ($SD = 14.23$). These two scores were used as indicators for the language construct.

Through use of a structural equation modeling approach, we demonstrated that language was positively related to a child's score on the Monopoly social problem-solving task ($z = 7.89$, $p < .0001$), indicating that greater language competence was directly related to better scores on the game-playing task. Greater three-year skill in both social communication with parents ($z = 4.91$, $p < .01$) and pretend play ($z = 3.05$; $p < .01$) also directly related to greater competence in six-year language skills. No significant correlations were found among the three-year constructs, although children with greater social communication skills tended to be somewhat more adept at solitary pretend

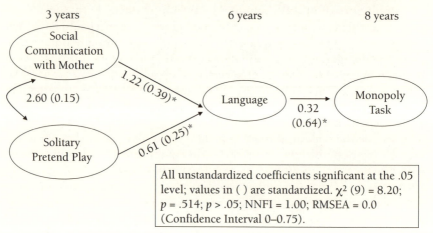

Figure 4.2. Estimated Relations Among Developmental Precursors and the Monopoly Social Problem-Solving Task Skills for Significant Paths Included in the Final Structural Model.

All unstandardized coefficients significant at the .05 level; values in ( ) are standardized. $\chi^2 (9) = 8.20$; $p = .514$; $p > .05$; NNFI = 1.00; RMSEA = 0.0 (Confidence Interval 0–0.75).

play ($z = 1.88$, $p < .10$). The model accounted for about 24% of the variance in the language construct and 10% of the social problem-solving construct (Figure 4.2). The potential indirect effects of the two three-year constructs on the problem-solving construct were next examined. Communication had a significant indirect effect on the problem-solving construct at eight years ($z = 4.49$, $p < .01$), as did pretend play ($z = 2.93$, $p < .05$). These indirect effects occurred through their direct effect on language at six years, which in turn supported children's ability to have effective social problem-solving skills.

It is theorized that children are not able to take experiences gained through pretend play scenarios and use them to make inferences about what other people know until they have developed the words that allow them to have those thoughts (Garfield, Peterson, & Perry, 2001). Thus the ability to use words becomes a central part of their cognitive development (Garfield et al., 2001). The results of our model lend some support to this notion because the influence of pretend play on sharing information with others was not direct, but rather moderated by later language skills. Early social communication skills may have a special importance for the later ability to solve problems with a partner because they afford the basic foundational skills governing the rules of social interaction (turn taking, reading the cues of another, following the sequence of conversation). These results suggest that many of these same skills need to be within the child's repertoire at later ages in order to function effectively in complex social situations with a partner other than a parent.

Summary. A major objective of this chapter was to present a novel, ecologically sensitive social problem-solving task for school-aged children (goal 1). The Rasch modeling of the behaviors involved in the Monopoly task involves many specific competencies important for children's ability to work with others (cognitive flexibility, reading a partner's social cues, describing procedures, accepting input from others, adapting communications). However, it is unique in the ability to capture one underlying developmental construct. In comparison to more traditional, standardized measures, the game-playing task appears more "ecologically valid" given that it is similar to everyday occurrences where children are required to use a range of cognitive and language skills to share information with others. The Monopoly task and scoring approach appears to be a valid measure of social problem solving during middle childhood; it predicted adolescents' ability to solve problems in situations with others such as peers and parents (goal 2). Finally, we demonstrated that it is the interrelation among early skills such as pretend play, social communication interactions with parents, and early school age language that are important precursors to middle childhood social problem solving rather than any one of these skills alone (goal 3).

Future directions for this work include the need to expand measurement approaches that place demands on children necessary for competence in social problem-solving situations. Furthering our knowledge of children's developing competencies in social situations requires understanding use of an integrated set of cognitive, language, and social skills in order to better understand social competence in everyday settings. The results described in this chapter demonstrate the power of considering these skills from a developmental perspective in a longitudinal design. They also reveal the potential for social interactions to be an important context for children to learn, with support from more competent others, how to solve social problems at later ages.

References

Achenbach, T. M., & Rescorla, L. A. (2001). *Manual for the ASEBA school-age forms & profiles.* Burlington: University of Vermont, Department of Psychiatry.

Andrich, D. (1988). *Rasch models for measurement.* Thousand Oaks, CA: Sage.

Astington, J. W., & Jenkins, J. M. (1999). A longitudinal study of the relation between language and theory-of-mind development. *Developmental Psychology, 35,* 1311–1320.

Astington J. W., & Pelletier, J. (2005). Theory of mind, language, and learning in the early years: Developmental origins of school readiness. In B. D. Homer & C. Tamis-Lemonda (Eds.), *The development of social cognition and communication* (pp. 205–231). Mahwah, NJ: Erlbaum.

Bretherton, I. (1984). Representing the social world in symbolic play: Reality and fantasy. In I. Bretherton (Ed.), *Symbolic play: The development of social understanding* (pp. 1–41). Orlando, FL: Academic Press.

Bruner, J. S. (1972). Nature and use of immaturity. *American Psychologist, 27,* 687–708.

Carlson, S. M., & Moses, L. J. (2001). Individual differences in inhibitory control and children's theory of mind. *Child Development, 72,* 1032–1053.

de Villiers, J. G., & Pyers, J. E. (2002). Complements to cognition: A longitudinal study of the relationship between complex syntax and false-belief-understanding. *Cognitive Development, 17,* 1037–1060.

Donaldson, M. (1978). *Children's minds.* Glasgow, Scotland: Fontana.

Eisenberg, N., Fabes, R. A., Guthrie, I. K., & Reiser, M. (2000). Dispositional emotionality and regulation: Their role in predicting quality of social functioning. *Journal of Personality and Social Psychology, 78,* 136–157.

Feldman, R., & Klein, P. S. (2003). Toddlers' self-regulated compliance to mothers, caregivers, and fathers: Implications for theories of socialization. *Developmental Psychology, 39,* 680–692.

Fenson, L., Kagan, J., Kearsley, R. B., & Zelazo, P. R. (1976). The developmental progression of manipulative play in the first two years. *Child Development, 47,* 232–236.

Fleiss, J. L. (1986). *The design and analysis of clinical experiments.* New York: Wiley.

Frick, T., & Semmel, M. (1978). Observer agreement and reliabilities of classroom observational methods. *Review of Educational Research, 48,* 157–184.

Garfield, J., Peterson, C., & Perry, T. (2001) Social cognition, language acquisition and the theory of mind. *Mind and Language, 16,* 494–541.

Halperin, J. M., Sharma, V., Greenblatt, E., & Schwartz, S. T. (1991). Assessment of the Continuous Performance Test reliability and validity in a nonreferred sample. *Psychological Assessment: A Journal of Consulting and Clinical Psychology, 3,* 603–608.

Hebert-Myers, H., Guttentag, C., Swank, P. R., Smith, K. E., & Landry, S. H. (2006). The importance of language, social, and behavioral skills across early and later childhood as predictors of social competence with peers. *Applied Developmental Science, 10,* 174–187.

Hughes, C. (1998). Finding your marbles: Does preschoolers' strategic behavior predict later understanding of mind? *Developmental Psychology, 34,* 1326–1339.

Imbens-Bailey, A. L., & Snow, C. E. (1997). Making meaning in parent-child interaction: A pragmatic approach. In C. Mandell & A. McCabe (Eds.), *The problem of meaning: Behavioral and cognitive perspectives* (pp. 261–295). Amsterdam, Netherlands: North-Holland Elsevier Science.

Isquith, P. K., Gioia, G. A., & Epsy, K. A. (2004). Executive function in preschool children: Examination through everyday behavior. *Developmental Neuropsychology, 26,* 403–422.

Keller, M., Edelstein, W., Schmid, C., Fang, F., & Fang, G. (1998). Reasoning about responsibilities and obligations in close relationships: A comparison across two cultures. *Developmental Psychology, 34,* 731–741.

Kim, J. K., Conger, R. D., Lorenz, F. O., & Elder, G. Jr. (2001). Parent-adolescent reciprocity in negative affect and its relation to early adult social development. *Developmental Psychology, 37,* 775–790.

Kochanska, G. (2002). Committed compliance, moral self, and internalization: A mediational model. *Developmental Psychology, 38,* 339–351.

Kochanska, G., & Murray, K. T. (2000). Mother-child mutually responsive orientation and conscience development: From toddler to early school age. *Child Development, 71,* 417–431.

Kuczynski, L., & Kochanska, G. (1995). Function and content of maternal demands: Developmental significance of early demands for competent action. *Child Development, 66,* 616–628.

Landry, S. H., Chapieski, M. L., Richardson, M. A., Palmer, J., & Hall, S. (1990). The social competence of children born prematurely: Effects of medical complications and parent behaviors. *Child Development, 61,* 1605–1616.

Landry, S. H., Miller-Loncar, C. L., Smith, K. E., & Swank, P. R. (2002). The role of parenting in children's development of executive processes. *Developmental Neuropsychology, 21,* 15–41.

Landry, S. H., Smith, K. E., & Swank, P. R. (2006). Responsive parenting: Establishing early foundations for social, communication, and independent problem solving. *Developmental Psychology, 42,* 627–642.

Landry, S. H., Smith, K. E., Swank, P. R., Assel, M. A., & Vellet, S. (2001). Does early responsive parenting have a special importance for children's development or is consistency across early childhood necessary? *Developmental Psychology, 37,* 387–403.

Landry, S. H., Smith, K. E., Swank, P. R., & Miller-Loncar, C. L. (2000). Early maternal and child influences on children's later independent cognitive and social functioning. *Child Development, 71*, 358–375.

Laursen, B., Coy, K. C., & Collins, W. A. (1998). Reconsidering changes in parent-child conflict across adolescence: A meta-analysis. *Child Development, 69*, 817–832.

Lezak, M. D. (1982). The problem of assessing executive functions. *International Journal of Psychology, 17*, 281–297.

Linacre, J. M. (1991–2004). A user's guide to winsteps ministep: Rasch modeling computer programs (computer software and manual). Retrieved from http://www.winsteps.com.

Loeber, R., Drinkwater, M., Yin, Y., Anderson, S. J., Schmidt, L. C., & Crawford, A. (2000). Stability of family interactions from ages 6 to 18. *Journal of Abnormal Child Psychology, 28*, 353–369.

McCune-Nicolich, L. (1981). Toward symbolic functioning: Structure of early pretend games and potential parallels with language. *Child Development, 52*, 785–797.

McGue, M., Elkins, I., Walden, B., & Iacono, W. G. (2005). Perceptions of the parent-adolescent relationship: A longitudinal investigation. *Developmental Psychology, 41*, 971–984.

Piaget, J. (1962). *Play, dreams, and imitation in childhood.* New York: Norton.

Raizner, R. D., Song, J., & Levin, H. S. (2002). Raising the ceiling: The Tower of London—extended version. *Developmental Neuropsychology, 21*, 1–14.

Reuter, M. A., & Conger, R. D. (1998). Reciprocal influences between parenting and adolescent problem-solving behavior. *Developmental Psychology, 34*, 1470–1482.

Rourke, B. P., & Fuerst, D. R. (1991). *Learning disabilities and psychosocial functioning: A neuropsychological perspective.* New York: Guilford Press.

Sattler, J. M. (2008). *Assessment of children: Cognitive foundations.* (5th Ed.) La Mesa, CA: Jerome M. Sattler.

Shallice, T. (1982). Specific impairments of planning. *Philosophical transactions of the Royal Society of London, 298*, 199–209.

Slomkowski, C., & Dunn, J. (1996). Young children's understanding of other people's beliefs and feelings and their connected communication with friends. *Developmental Psychology, 32*, 442–447.

Snow, C. E. (1999). Social perspectives on the emergence of language. In B. MacWhinney (Ed.), *The emergence of language* (pp. 257–276). Mahwah, NJ: Erlbaum.

Steinberg, L. (2005). *Adolescence.* (7th Ed.) New York: McGraw-Hill.

Steinberg, L., Dahl, R., Keating, D., Kupfer, D. J., Masten, A. S., & Pine, D. (2006). The study of developmental psychopathology in adolescence: Integrating affective neuroscience with the study of context. In D. Cicchetti & D. Cohen (Eds.), *Developmental psychopathology* (2nd Ed.; pp. 710–741). Hoboken, NJ: Worldcat.

Thorndike, R. L., Hagen, E. P., & Sattler, J. M. (1986). *Guide for administering and scoring the Stanford-Binet Intelligence Scale: 4th edition.* Chicago: Riverside.

Tomasello, M., Kruger, A. C., & Ratner, H. H. (1993). Cultural learning. *Behavioral and Brain Sciences, 16*, 495–552.

Welsch, M. C., & Pennington, B. F. (1988). Assessing frontal lobe functioning in children: Views from developmental psychology. *Developmental Neuropsychology, 4*, 199–230.

Wenxin, Z., Meiping, W., & Fuligni, A. (2006). Expectations for autonomy, beliefs about parental authority, and parent-adolescent conflict and cohesion. *Acta Psychologica Sinica, 38*, 868–876.

Wiig, E. H., Secord, W., & Semel, E. (1992). *Clinical Evaluation of Language Fundamentals—Preschool Edition.* San Antonio, TX: Psychological Corporation.

Wolf, D. P., Rygh, J., & Altshuler, J. (1984). Agency and experience: Actions and states in play narratives. In I. Bretherton (Ed.), *Symbolic play: The development of social understanding* (pp. 195–217). New York: Academic Press.

Appendix

This table gives examples of queries used by examiners in the Monopoly game task.

Rule Number	Level 1 Query	Level 2 Query	Level 3 Query
1. Select a car or color	What do I do now?	What do we do with the car?	Should we pick a car?
4. Start on "Go"	How do we start?	What is this space for?	Should we start on "Go"?
7. Move what you roll	Now what?	How do I know how many to move?	Maybe I should move the number on the dice?
10. Chance: draw a card	What's that?	What should I do with the card?	Maybe I should pick up a chance card?
12. Railroad: roll again	What do I do here?	What should I do with the dice?	Should I roll again?
14. Uncle Pig (take money)	What do I do here?	What do we do here with this money?	Does the person who lands here get the money?
15. Rest rooms	Now what?	What should I do when I land here?	Should I just do nothing?

SUSAN H. LANDRY *is the Michael Matthew Knight Professor of Pediatrics at the University of Texas Health Science Center, Houston.*

KAREN E. SMITH *is professor of neurology, obstetrics and gynecology, and pediatrics at the University of Texas Medical Branch, Galveston.*

PAUL R. SWANK *is professor of pediatrics at the University of Texas Health Science Center.*

Lewis, C., Koyasu, M., Oh, S., Ogawa, A., Short, B., & Huang, Z. (2009). Culture, executive function, and social understanding. In C. Lewis & J. I. M. Carpendale (Eds.), Social interaction and the development of executive function. *New Directions in Child and Adolescent Development, 123,* 69–85.

Culture, Executive Function, and Social Understanding

Charlie Lewis, Masuo Koyasu, Seungmi Oh, Ayako Ogawa, Benjamin Short, Zhao Huang

Abstract

Much of the evidence from the West has shown links between children's developing self-control (executive function), their social experiences, and their social understanding (Carpendale & Lewis, 2006, chapters 5 and 6), across a range of cultures including China. This chapter describes four studies conducted in three Oriental cultures, suggesting that the relationships among social interaction, executive function, and social understanding are different in these cultures, implying that social and executive skills are underpinned by key cultural processes. © Wiley Periodicals, Inc.

If executive function has a basis in social interaction, then we should see the effects of cultural differences in performance. In this chapter, the focus is on this buoyant research tradition in relation to another, even more active area: children's grasp of the social world. This research has recently come under the banner of "theory of mind" (e.g., Perner, 1991; Wellman, 1990). It centers on the understanding that our minds work independently of events in the world. Over the past 25 years, the main assessment of the ability to understand this fact comes from a group of tasks known as "false belief" tests.

False belief tasks are simply defined. Suppose a story character places a toy in one location and then, while she is out, another person moves it elsewhere. The story character now has a false belief. In the task, the child has to predict where that character will look or where she will think an object is as she returns for the toy. The research evidence suggests that children acquire this ability sometime around their fourth birthday, with slight cultural variations (Wellman, Cross, & Watson, 2001). Although there is general concern that the field relies too much on false belief tasks (Astington, 2001), this test remains a dominant one in research.

We focus on recent research links that have been made between social understanding in general and false belief understanding in particular with executive functions (Schneider, Schumann-Hengsteler, & Sodian, 2005), language (Astington & Baird, 2005), and many linked social processes such as the structure of the child's social networks and the parents' interaction styles (Ruffman, Perner, & Parkin 1999). Carpendale and Lewis (2006) provide an integrated review on how these factors interrelate. The aim is to explore whether an analysis of culture can help us not only grasp the relationship between two empirical constructs, false belief understanding and executive function, but also consider the role of culture in forming these skills.

The Role of Culture

Why might culture be important? We consider the term both with reference to different societies, and in how everyday experiences and practices may be crucial in development of human skills (Tomasello, Kruger, & Ratner, 1993). There are many reasons executive function should be subject to cultural analysis. One obvious setting to conduct comparative research in is Northeast Asia, where children exhibit notable patterns of self-control in their interactions with others (Tobin, Wu, & Davidson, 1989). Even though Eastern cultures have become increasingly Westernized (Tobin, Karasawa, & Hsueh, 2004), children, particularly in Confucian societies,[1] continue to show more self-control than their Western counterparts (see, e.g., Sabbagh, Xu, Carlson, Moses, & Lee, 2006). At the same time, research on children's social understanding has suggested that Western children might have a slight head start in crucial developments in tests of false belief understanding (Wellman et al., 2001), particularly over children from Japan. The link between executive function and social understanding has received much theoretical analysis; the aim here is to explore two leading accounts in order to suggest a need for more detailed analyses of the nature of executive function in oriental children. This, it is hoped, will illuminate the broad influence of social interaction on social and executive skills via the lens of cultural practices.

The motivation for the research came from our observations and analyses of the skills of preschoolers in three cultures: Korea, Japan, and China. For example, Oh and Lewis (2008) described the literature on Korean children's behavior in preschools. We found a number of reports of the children's conduct in preschool settings seeming to support the idea that children in Northeast Asia behave differently from those in the West. Even three-year-olds spend up to an hour per session performing whole-class activities (Kwon, 2002), often receiving formal instruction (French & Song, 1998). Teachers simply use attention-grabbing procedures to maintain children's interest and thus draw on and encourage the child's executive function skills so that they pay attention and sit relatively still. Similar patterns are reported in other oriental cultures. For example, in China parents (Chao & Tseng, 2002) and teachers (Wang & Mao, 1996) stress the importance of filial respect and self-control in everyday conduct. A major question concerns whether such observed patterns of behavior influence the preschooler's developing cognitive control and grasp of social interactions. This allows us to address questions about the three-way links among these skills, given the types of social interactions that are manifest in particular cultural practices.

The chapter is divided into two main sections. In the first, we briefly describe two claims that are made about development of executive function skills: that children's grasp of the social world is founded on their capacity for self-control, and that both sets of skills are themselves linked to factors in the child's social environment. The second section explores each claim by testing two questions that emerge from the Western literature. We answer both questions by drawing on our data from the three oriental cultures of Korea, Japan, and China.

Social Interactions, Executive Function, and Social Understanding in Oriental Children: Emerging Questions

How do these three factors relate to each other? The literature tends to focus on two of the three possible relationships: between executive function and false belief understanding and between social interactions and social understanding.

Executive Function and False Belief. The evidence from Western studies has increasingly suggested that theory of mind is closely related to executive function (Carlson, Moses, & Breton, 2002; Frye, Zelazo, & Palfai, 1995; Hala, Hug, & Henderson, 2003; Hughes, 1998a; Perner, Lang, &

Kloo, 2002). There is much discussion about a possible causal relationship between these two abilities, from the claim that an understanding of internal states assists self-control (Perner & Lang, 2000) to the idea that something about executive function is necessary for social understanding. This "something" includes working memory (Davis & Pratt, 1995; Gordon & Olson, 1998), the ability to embed rules within an overall framework (Frye et al., 1995), and inhibitory control (Carlson & Moses, 2001; Carlson et al., 2002; Carlson, Moses, & Hix, 1998; Hala et al., 2003; Russell, 1996).

The debate on the relationship between executive functioning and social understanding continues apace. There is some evidence for the claim that the two skills are functionally interdependent. Kloo and Perner (2003) trained children either in executive skills (more specifically, assessing set shifting), as measured by the Dimensional Change Card Sort (DCCS) procedure (Frye et al., 1995), or false belief understanding. They found that training on one skill led to improved performance on the other. We have replicated this in our laboratory (Short, 2007). However, a more consistent stream of research suggests that executive function underpins social understanding. For example, both microgenetic (Flynn, O'Malley, & Wood, 2004) and longitudinal (Hughes, 1998b) studies have found that executive skills predict later false belief understanding. There are some claims for a general link between executive skills and false belief, but more specifically Carlson and Moses's studies have produced correlations between inhibitory control and mental state understanding (usually false belief understanding, but also deception) that remain significant even when other factors such as language are taken into consideration (Carlson et al., 2002; Carlson et al., 1998; Hala et al., 2003). These analyses lead to the first question that we address in the next section: whether the executive function can be shown to underpin social understanding across a range of oriental cultures, as predicted by the bulk of Western data (Moses & Sabbagh, 2007).

Social Interaction and Social Understanding. It has been increasingly asserted that children's social experience is associated with their social understanding (e.g., Carpendale et al., 2004; Hughes & Leekam, 2004). Children's social networks allow them access to social knowledge and possibly self-control. Three particular influences have been examined, namely siblings, parents and careers, and peers. The "sibling effect" (see Carpendale & Lewis, 2006, chapter 6) has received closest attention (Perner, Ruffman, & Leekam, 1994; Ruffman, Perner, Naito, Parkin, & Clements, 1998) and shows (although not universally; Cutting & Dunn, 1999; Peterson & Slaughter, 2003) that a child's false belief skills are correlated with the number of siblings. Other research shows that the number of siblings is also related to executive function performance in preschoolers (Cole & Mitchell, 2000).

However, the picture is more complex. First, there are reports that the presence of older kin and the frequency of the child's interactions with kin correlated with her or his false belief performance as strongly as the number of siblings (Lewis, Freeman, Kyriakidou, Maridaki-Kassotaki, & Berridge, 1996). Second, parental style has been reported to influence preschoolers' social development. A fourfold typology of parenting styles has been used: indulgent, authoritarian, authoritative, and uninvolved (Maccoby & Martin, 1983), based on studies of families in the West. Authoritative parents are construed as more successful because the strategy of setting standards within a relationship of trust and negotiation helps the child develop self-regulation (Baumrind, 1991). Ruffman et al. (1999) designed a short questionnaire to assess how parents' responses to real or hypothetical transgressions by the child correlated with the child's false belief understanding. They found that Western mothers who would ask their child to reflect on the victim's feelings (or "how feel," HF, responses) had preschoolers with more advanced skills. This effect was independent of the sibling effect. Third, preschoolers who played with peers more in shared pretence and cooperation (Lalonde & Chandler, 1995) were also more likely to achieve an earlier grasp of false belief.

These factors give rise to our second question, concerning the three-way relationship among culture, executive function, and social understanding. It asks whether these patterns of influence are in evidence in Confucian cultures. There are grounds for assuming that they are not. For example, on the issue of parenting styles, Vinden (2001) found the predicted pattern of authoritarian parenting being negatively related to social understanding in European American families, but not found in Korean American families.

Question 1: Does EF Predict Unique Variance in Performance on False Belief?

The literature reports a consistency in findings on the relationship between executive function performance and social understanding across diverse cultures, including Africa, South America, and Europe (Chasiotis, Kiessling, Winter, & Hofer, 2006) and China (Sabbagh et al., 2006). It may seem unnecessary to conduct research in another culture in order to test the claim once more. However, we decided to test the closeness of the association in Korea, given the points made above that this is a culture steeped in a Confucian tradition stressing interdependence between individuals, involving respect for others and keen obedience to authority figures such as parents and teachers.

Self-Control in Korean Culture. Even within new-generation American families (Farver & Lee-Shin, 2000; Parmar, Harkness, & Super, 2004), Asian cultures emphasize the role of academic training over play in children. Preschools within Korea display adherence to traditional collectivist values, despite their reference to "child-centered" influences from Western philosophies (Kwon, 2002). Kwon's research shows that, in fact, teachers prefer to run class-based activities in which a high degree of self-control in the child is expected.

A very clear insight into just how different Korean preschools are from those in the West comes from French and Song's observational study (1998). They offer detailed accounts of how children as young as three years perform such class-based activities as sitting and attending for up to an hour per day, with few showing any signs of fidgeting. The teachers seemed very proficient at gaining the children's attention and maintaining their interest, even though the subject matter of lessons was detailed. The explicit aim of such teaching is to encourage listening and concentration skills. The key issue is whether such training at school and at home has any impact on the level of self-control that would be predicted from an account that stresses the role of social interaction in development of executive skills.

The Korean Studies: Research Design. In our first experiment (see Oh et al., 2008, for more detail), we administered a battery of executive skills and false belief tasks taken from Western studies to 40 three- and four-year-olds from professional families in Seoul. The age range was restricted to three years six months and four years six months; the aim was to get a feel for the level of performance in tests of working memory (the Eight Boxes Scrambled task and Backward Word Span), inhibitory control (Luria's Hand Game and Day-Night), delay inhibition (Tower Building and Gift Delay), and set shifting (the Dimension Change Card Sort, or DCCS). In brief:

- The Eight Boxes task involves the child retrieving a sticker from each one of eight boxes, clearly distinguished by color and pattern, but they are moved around between each child's selection of a new box.
- Backward Word Span requires the child to recall increasingly large list of words in reverse order.
- Over a series of trials, in Luria's Hand Game the child has to produce the other hand shape when the tester demonstrates either a fist or a point.
- In the Day-Night test the child has to say "Day" when a picture of the moon with stars is turned over and "Night" when a picture of the sun is revealed.
- Tower Building requires the child to take turns in building a tower with an experimenter who is slightly slow in placing her blocks in a stack in which the child and she take turns; the child's failure to take turns is measured.
- Gift delay involves placing an invited wrapped gift in front of the child and seeing whether and how long it takes for a child to open it even though the child has been asked to wait to do so (see Oh & Lewis, 2008 for a full description).

The Korean Studies: Results. The patterns of these Korean data were at odds with those of studies using the same measures with Western children of a similar age. Figure 5.1 presents the performance on those tests in which a percentage score out of the maximum possible could be calculated. It shows that most of these children, even the three-year-olds, were near or at ceiling on these measures. There were exceptions in that on the delay tasks children failed to take turns and stack bricks to make a tower, but the performance in Figure 5.1 does not reveal that 72% were at ceiling; they waited for 150 seconds without touching an enticing gift, while the average score was lowered by a small minority who acted impetuously. On a final

Figure 5.1. Performance of Three- and Four-Year-Olds on Six Executive Function Tests in Experiment 1.

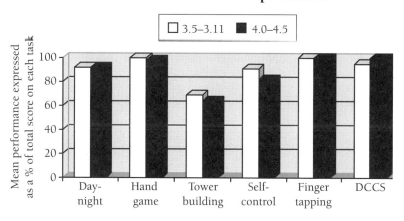

measure, Backward Word Span, the child had to repeat a list of words in the reverse order. The span was 1.65 for three-year-olds and 2.25 for the four-year-olds, which compares favorably with similar measures taken from Western children (e.g., Davis et al., 1995) but is not at the ceiling.

Two further findings are noteworthy from this experiment. First, the children did not show these precocious levels of performance in false belief tests. In both groups, 31–38% of children passed the critical test question about the protagonist's false beliefs in two questions from the same deceptive box test: after the child has been shown that a chocolate box actually contains pencils the child is asked what he or she thought, and what a friend will think, is inside. Second, only one measure, Backward Word Span, correlated with a score of Total False Belief ($r = .3$), but this became nonsignificant when a test of language skill was taken into account. However, this study did not compare children from a Western culture with those in Korea, and the age range was somewhat narrow. We therefore carried out a second study comparing Korean and British children.

In study 2, we compared 76 three- and four-year-old Korean children with 64 English preschoolers of the same age, ranging between their third and fifth birthdays. We administered a battery of tests like those in study 1, but we wanted to avoid the problem of failing to find associations between the executive function measures and false belief because the former measures were almost at ceiling in the first study. If this were the case, then failure to find an association with false belief could simply be the result of a lack of variance in one or both types of measure. We thus used more complex tasks including one, Blue-Red, that coauthor Seungmi Oh devised for the purpose of providing a more exacting test. In this task, the child has to put an index finger on a red square of paper when the experimenter says

Figure 5.2. Performance of the Four Age Groups of Korean (Dotted Bars) and English (Plain Bars) Children on Two Executive Tests, Expressed as a Proportion of All Trials.

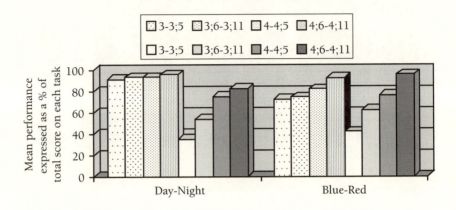

"blue" and a blue square when she says "red." Over a series of trials, this measures conflict inhibition (the ability to resist the temptation to touch blue when the experimenter says "blue"), like the Luria hand game or Day-Night tasks.

The results replicated study 1 at least in part. Figure 5.2 presents the levels of performance in each of the four six-month periods between three and almost five. The four bars with dotted backgrounds show the data for the Korean age subgroups, while the bars on the right with the plain backgrounds show the comparable data for the English children. On the left of Figure 5.2 the data show that for the Day-Night test the Korean children were nearly at ceiling, even in those under three and a half years, who did better than English children almost two years older than them. In contrast the young English children performed at a much lower level and even the oldest English children were not as good as the youngest Koreans. On other measures, like the Blue-Red task shown on the right of Figure 5.2, the Korean children were not at ceiling. However, the younger Koreans tended to show higher levels of performance than their English counterparts and there was less steep improvement with age.

Unlike in study 1, the false belief performance showed a linear increase by age group in the two cultures, but no influence of culture. For example, in the unexpected transfer false belief test, in which the child should predict that a protagonist will act on his outdated beliefs rather than current reality, performance increased from 10% in young Korean three-year-olds (three to three and a half) to 59% in those in the second half of the fifth year of life. The comparable data for the English sample were 0% and 69% for these age groups. Given that the tests of executive function did not show ceiling effects across the board, we conducted a series of analyses to explore whether the age-related changes in executive function relate to these clear developments in false belief performance. We present here an analysis in which we standardized each executive test and then extracted a general score of executive performance, following the procedure employed by Sabbagh et al. (2006). They then regressed false belief performance onto this composite measure while taking into account the child's age, gender, and scores on a general language measure to control for the child's verbal IQ.

Table 5.1 presents the findings of Sabbagh et al. followed by those obtained in study 2. Sabbagh and colleagues found a higher level of performance in tests of executive function in a sample of preschoolers from Beijing over a matched sample in the United States. They found, despite these differences in executive performance, that this group of tests predicted false belief equally well, even when the control measures were partialed out (see the righthand column of Table 5.1). When we carried out a similar analysis on our data, we found that the data from the UK matched those of Sabbagh et al. However, in Korea the picture appeared to be different. There was only a moderate link between the composite executive function and false belief scores ($r(69) = .34$, $p < .005$, compared with $r(51) = .56$, $p < .001$, for the English sample), which became nonsignificant once verbal mental age and chronological age were taken into account (see Table 1). Thus the Korean data do not appear to support the idea of a relationship between social understanding (as measured by false belief) and a range of executive function tests.

Executive Function and Social Understanding in Other Northeast Asian Cultures. The difference between the Korean and Chinese data prompted study 3. In it we examined whether the pattern of findings obtained in Korea was atypical of findings in the East. We tested 87 Japanese and 81 English three- to five-year-old children. The age range was extended because Japanese children have been reported to lag behind their Western counterparts on false belief tasks. For example, Naito and Koyama (2006) found that false belief tests were not reliably passed until the children were at least six years old.

The children were given two false belief tasks (unexpected transfer and the deceptive box) and these executive tests: Luria's Hand Game, the Blue-Red task to measure conflict inhibition, Tower Building for delay inhibition, Backward Word Span and Eight Boxes Scrambled to assess working memory, and the Dimensional Change Card Sort to measure set shifting. The results were closer to those we found in Korea than Sabbagh et al.'s Chinese data. We followed their procedures and for each set of tests constructed a composite score for both executive function and false belief. As with the Korean data, the two composite measures correlated with one another ($r(68) = .38$, $p < 01$ and $r(81) = .5$, $p < 001$, respectively, for the Japanese and English data). However, once chronological and verbal age were taken into consideration the English data remained significant while the correlation in the Japanese study was approximately zero (see Table 5.1).

Table 5.1. Comparison Between Four Studies in Which False Belief Scores Are Regressed Onto an Executive Function Composite Measure, Showing the Size of the Model (R^2) and the Correlation of Executive Function and False Belief Once Background Variables Are Partialed Out.

Study/Sample	R^2 Significance	EF-False Belief Partial Correlation (Age, Sex, VMA Controlled)
Sabbagh et al. (2006)		
China	.35, $p < .001$	$r = .393, p < .01$
United States	.4, $p < .001$	$r = .366, p < .01$
Oh and Lewis data		
Korea	.24, $p < .001$	$r = -.012$, NS
UK	.37, $p < .001$	$r = .379, p < .01$
Lewis, Koyasu, Ogawa, and Short data		
Japan	.24, $p < .001$	$r = .018$, NS
UK	.26, $p < .001$	$r = .356, p < .01$
Lewis, Zhao, and Rooksby data		
China	.05, NS	$r = .141$, NS

Finally we conducted study 4 in China (for full details, see Lewis, Huang, & Rooksby, 2006). The full aims of this study are described later. We must be cautious about these data because we conducted a limited range of executive function measures, but we feel we should report the results here for completeness. We tested a sample of 75 three- to five-year-olds in Zhuhai, a city of one million inhabitants in the southern Chinese province of Guangdong. The children were given four executive tests: Luria's Hand Game, Blue-Red, DCCS, and Backward Word Span. Table 5.1 presents the results of the analyses we conducted to make them comparable with the other studies. The raw correlation between the executive function and false belief composites was weak and of borderline significance ($r(67) = .23, p = .06$). When the same background variables were added to a regression analysis, the model was not significant. So in these Chinese data the link between executive function as a whole and false belief is not to be found, matching the findings of the Korean and Japanese comparisons with the UK.

As we stated in the introduction to this chapter, it might be the case that although executive functions in general might not show the expected correlations with false belief (see Table 5.1), there are specific links between these two sets of skills. In that section we reviewed some of the literature suggesting that conflict inhibition and working memory best predict false belief performance. We looked for such specific links in these databases and found some support for a conflict inhibition–false belief correlation. However, when age in the Chinese study and verbal skills in the Japanese and Korean studies were taken into account, these links were no longer significant. We therefore conclude that this pattern, like the general one explored earlier, is apparent in preschoolers in the West but is not easily identifiable in these oriental samples.

Question 2: Does the Social Environment Predict Performance on False Belief and Executive Tests?

Chinese Parenting and the Child's Social Network. The Chinese study already described had another central focus of attention. China's "one-child" policy, which is adhered to by the vast majority of urban families, was the main focus of our attention because it allows us to explore more closely the role of culture in development of social understanding, particularly the sibling effect described in the introduction.

Exploring Children's Access to Key Social Interactions in China. The one-child policy has been adhered to in most urban families. It makes the Chinese family very different from those in the West (and indeed other oriental cultures) and allows us to test the claim we made (Lewis et al., 1996) that kin relationships may have a similar impact on social understanding and executive skill as do sibling relationships in Western cultures. We hypothesised that the Chinese one-child policy has a bearing on both the number of socially skilled family members the child interacts with and the parents' psychological investment in, and reaction to, the single child.

We also explored the nature of the child's social network and the parents' styles of interaction. The study was an attempt to explore whether the correlations found in Western studies between authoritative parenting and social understanding could be generalized to this very different cultural setting. For the 75 children tested, 64 parents returned questionnaires with information about the child's daily contact with kin and the parent's (predominantly the mother's) attitude toward her responses to the child's acts.

To obtain detailed information about their children's social networks, parents were asked to report (1) how many people live with the child, (2) how many older and younger cousins live in the same city, (3) the child's contact with these cousins, (4) contact with friends, (5) parent-child contact during the week and on the weekend, and (6) the child's contact with babysitters. To examine parenting style, we adapted the 1999 questionnaire from Ruffman et al. for use in Chinese culture but report here only the four overlapping categories. The parent was asked how he or she reacted to events where child had shouted at the parent, lied, hit someone, or taken something. Four types of parental reaction are coded: (1) encouraging the child to reflect on the emotional perspective of the victim of the transgression (the "how feel" response mentioned earlier); (2) explaining or exploring the situation in some way without referring to the victim's feelings ("general discussion" responses); (3) disciplining the child, scored as a "reprimand"; and (4) "ambiguous," involving both reprimand and general discussion responses (Ruffman et al., 1999).

The Findings. The size of the Chinese household resembled that in the West. The children lived with an average of three other people, ranging from lone parent households to those with seven other family members (even if none included siblings). More than half had at least one cousin within the city, and there was sufficient variability in the measures of frequency of contact and play with them and peers to allow correlational analyses. The parenting questionnaires revealed differences from those obtained by Ruffman et al. in England. In their study, the modal response was to the child's infringement with a reprimand (64%), while in this Chinese sample the majority (69%) of response was general discussion, without explicit mention of the other's feelings. Only a few mentioned how the victim felt (10%) or used a reprimand (3%), while a further 18% were categorized as ambiguous—containing both a reprimand and discussion about the event without mentioning the other's feelings (compared with 7% in the Ruffman et al. sample). It is tempting to conclude that such differences reflect popular discussion about the Chinese one-child policy promoting "indulgent" parenting and thus "spoilt" children (Taylor, 2005). The low level of reported reprimands and higher rate of ambiguous responses testify to this. However, detailed analyses of actual interactions and their long-term correlates would be required to support such a view.

How closely did these social factors relate to the child's executive function and false belief test performance? None of the social interaction or parenting measures was significantly correlated with a composite executive function score, and tentative follow-up analysis revealed that only working memory correlated with one measure—a composite of the size of the child's social network including the numbers of individuals in contact with the child—but here the relationship was negative ($r(63) = -.26$, $p < .05$). Given that overall family size is often a proxy for social status, this result suggests that the child's social interaction may not, in this sample or cultural setting, relate to her or his executive functions.

There were significant links between social relationships and social understanding. Two related to false belief: the number of older cousins that a child has and the frequency of play with cousins. In both cases the effect was negative, thus yielding an effect in the opposite direction to the sibling effect reported in the literature on Western children.

General Discussion

One aim of this chapter has been to reflect on data from three oriental cultures in order to draw some general conclusions about the role of social interactions in executive functions and social understanding. The answers to both questions suggest that the patterns of executive skills and their correlates with standard false belief measures are very different from those found in Western cultures. As Steven Tulkin pointed out long ago, such contrasts between different societies are sufficient to produce culture shock, to jolt us out of a set of assumptions that we see as invariant simply because our observation of similar Western cultures suggests they are. In this section we briefly reflect on why oriental children seem to be so good at executive tasks, why this advantage does not appear to carry over to a grasp of social understanding, and why both these sets of abilities do not seem to relate in the same way to social processes as they do in the West.

First, why do oriental children exhibit greater control over their actions than Western children? The answer is that we do not exactly know, because there are so many possibilities. As Sabbagh et al. (2006) suggest, the differences could be attributed to genetic factors because there are cultural differences in markers for disorders in executive control (Chang, Kidd, Livak, Pakastis, & Kidd, 1996), but the leap to typical development may be premature. A cultural explanation may receive more support, but even here we cannot specify how this would operate. We argued in the introduction that early education policies might stress the role of self-control in preschoolers' everyday conduct (e.g., Tobin et al., 1989). However, culture is a complete package. A brief look at one culture, Korea, illustrates this point. This shows that there are other factors such as the demands parents make in terms of filial duty (see Park & Cheah, 2005, for an analysis of Korea), or the fact that early parental speech to preschoolers contains action verbs (Choi & Bowerman, 1991), which might facilitate or emphasize the role of control in early behavior.

The second issue relates to the lack of an association in these studies between executive function and social understanding (see Table 5.1). There are two possible explanations that require further investigation. The first is that the measures of both processes might not easily translate from one cultural setting to another and that measures should be adapted to each specific locale. It might be the case, for example, that the superior performance shown in Korean children in Table 5.1 reflects advantages in some executive skills, but others might show no such advantages. Measures of these other skills might correlate with tests of social understanding. Similarly, standard false belief measures may underestimate the social understanding skills of children in oriental cultures, especially Japan. Close attention must always be paid to the calibration of measures across cultures, and we used tests to produce sufficient variability in Eastern cultures for comparison with false belief to be valid (and in the Blue-Red case devised a test of conflict inhibition to make this possible). We thus feel that the data presented here are sufficient to question whether accounts of the relationship between the two sets of skills in the West can be generalized to all cultural settings. Indeed it could be the case, as Kloo and Perner's training studies (2003) might suggest, that the links are caused by other, culture-specific underlying factors, among them the child's ability to comprehend an experimenter's instructions.

The third issue concerns the role of specific social factors. The answer to our second question is that to an extent factors in the Chinese child's social environment do predict their social understanding and executive function, but in the opposite direction to the ones predicted in Western studies; for example, we found that more contact with extended family members and siblings independently correlated with false belief in Greece, but the cousins–false belief association was negative in China. Far from enhancing the child's performance, the presence of and interactions with kin appear to have, if anything, a detrimental effect on these developmental measures. We are not arguing that this is necessarily a casual relationship. It might be the case that in a culture of singletons children might find relationships with proximal kin difficult, but such inferences need much further testing. However, the data presented here can be taken together to show how cross-cultural differences are used to question assumptions about links taken to be universal in one cultural setting. More important, they pinpoint the need for deeper analyses of the processes within differing cultures, which might give rise to the sorts of difference hinted at here.

Note

1. Confucius (551–479 B.C.) was a Chinese thinker and philosopher. His teachings have deeply influenced Chinese, Korean, and Japanese societies and cultures. Although Confucianism is often taken as a religion, it lacks the concepts of afterlife and spirituality. It is, so to speak, an ethical philosophy. Confucius' principles gained wide acceptance until the 19th century in Northeast Asian countries. However, its influence has been diminishing, especially in industrialized and urbanized areas. Korea is the country in which Confucius' tradition has been most preserved.

References

Astington, J. W. (2001). The future of theory-of-mind research: Understanding motivational states, the role of language, and real-world consequences. *Child Development, 72,* 685–687.
Astington, J. W., & Baird, J. A. (Eds.). (2005). *Why language matters for theory of mind.* New York: Oxford University Press.
Baumrind, D. (1991). Parenting styles and adolescent development. In R. M. Lerner, A. C. Petersen, & J. Brooks-Gunn (Eds.), *Encyclopedia of Adolescence* (Vol. 2). New York: Garland.
Carlson, S. M., & Moses, L. J. (2001). Individual differences in inhibitory control and children's theory of mind. *Child Development, 72,* 1032–1053.
Carlson, S. M., Moses, L. J., & Breton, C. (2002). How specific is the relation between executive function and theory of mind? Contribution of inhibitory control and working memory. *Infant and Child Development, 11,* 73–92.
Carlson, S. M., Moses, L. J., & Hix, H. R. (1998). The role of inhibitory control in young children's difficulties with deception and false belief. *Child Development, 69,* 672–691.
Carpendale, J. I. M., & Lewis, C. (2004). Constructing an understanding of mind. *Behavioral and Brain Sciences, 27,* 79–151.
Carpendale, J. I. M., & Lewis, C. (2006). *How children develop social understanding.* Oxford, England: Blackwell.

Chang, F.-M., Kidd, J. R., Livak, K. J., Pakastis, A. J., & Kidd, K. K. (1996). The worldwide distribution of allele frequencies at the human dopamine D4 receptor locus. *Human Genetics, 98*, 91–101.
Chao, R., & Tseng, V. (2002). Parenting of Asians. In M. Bornstein (Ed.), *Handbook of parenting. Volume 4: Social conditions and applied parenting* (2nd Ed., pp. 59–93). Mahwah, NJ: Erlbaum.
Chasiotis, A., Kiessling, F., Winter, V., & Hofer, J. (2006). Sensory motor inhibition as a prerequisite for theory of mind: A comparison of clinical and normal preschoolers differing in sensory motor abilities. *International Journal of Behavioral Development, 30*, 178–190.
Choi, S., & Bowerman, M. (1991). Learning to express motion events in English and Korean: The influence of language-specific lexicalization patterns. *Cognition, 41*, 83–121.
Cole, K., & Mitchell, P. (2000). Siblings in the development of executive control and a theory of mind. *British Journal of Developmental Psychology, 18*, 279–295.
Cutting, A. L., & Dunn, J. (1999). Theory of mind, emotion understanding, language, and family background: Individual differences and interrelations. *Child Development, 70*, 853–865.
Davis, H. L., & Pratt, C. (1995). The development of children's theory of mind: The working memory explanation. *Australian Journal of Psychology, 47*, 25–31.
Farver, J.A.M., & Lee-Shin, Y. (2000). Acculturation and Korean-American children's social and play behavior. *Social Development, 9*, 316–336.
Flynn, E., O'Malley, C., & Wood, D. (2004). A longitudinal, microgenetic study of the emergence of false belief understanding and inhibition skills. *Developmental Science, 7*, 103–115.
French, L., & Song, M. (1998). Developmentally appropriate teacher-directed approaches: Images from Korean kindergartens. *Journal of Curriculum Studies, 30*, 409–430.
Frye, D., Zelazo, P. D., & Palfai, T. (1995). Theory of mind and rule-based reasoning. *Cognitive Development, 10*, 483–527.
Gordon, A.C.L., & Olson, D. R. (1998). The relation between acquisition of a theory of mind and the capacity to hold in mind. *Journal of Experimental Child Psychology, 68*, 70–83.
Hala, S., Hug, S., & Henderson, A. (2003). Executive function and false-belief understanding in preschool children: Two tasks are harder than one. *Journal of Cognition and Development, 4*, 275–298.
Happaney, K., & Zelazo, P. D. (2003). Inhibition as a problem in the psychology of behavior. *Developmental Science, 6*, 468–470.
Hughes, C. (1998a). Executive function in preschoolers: Links with theory of mind and emotion and verbal ability. *British Journal of Developmental Psychology, 16*, 233–253.
Hughes, C. (1998b). Finding your marbles: Does preschoolers' strategic behavior predict later understanding of mind? *Developmental Psychology, 34*, 1326–1339.
Hughes, C., & Leekam, S. (2004). What are the links between theory of mind and social relations? Review, reflections and new directions for studies of typical and atypical development. *Social Development, 13*, 598–619.
Kloo, D., & Perner, J. (2003). Training transfer between card sorting and false belief understanding: Helping children apply conflicting descriptions. *Child Development, 74*, 1823–1839.
Kwon, Y.-I. (2002). Western influences in Korean preschool education. *International Education Journal, 3*, 153–164.
Lalonde, C. E., & Chandler, M. J. (1995). False belief understanding goes to school: On the social-emotional consequences of coming early or late to a first theory of mind. *Cognition and Emotion, 9*, 167–185.
Lewis, C., Freeman, N., Kyriakidou, C., Maridaki-Kassotaki, K., & Berridge, D. (1996). Social influences on false belief access. *Child Development, 67*, 2930–2947.

Lewis, C., Huang, Z., & Rooksby, M. (2006). Chinese preschoolers' false belief understanding: Is social knowledge underpinned by parental styles, social interactions or executive functions? *Psychologia, 49,* 252–266.
Maccoby, E. E., & Martin, J. A. 1983. Socialization in the context of the family: Parent-child interaction. In P. H. Mussen (Ed.) & E. M. Hetherington (Vol. Ed.), *Handbook of child psychology: Vol. 4. Socialization, personality, and social development* (4th ed., pp. 1–101). New York: Wiley.
Moses, L. J., & Sabbagh, M. A. (2007). Interactions between domain general and domain specific processes in the development of children's theories of mind. In M. J. Roberts (Ed.), *Integrating the mind: Domain general versus domain specific processes in higher cognition* (pp. 375–391). Hove, England: Psychology Press.
Naito, M., & Koyama, K. (2006). The development of false belief understanding in Japanese children: Delay and difference? *International Journal of Behavioral Development, 30,* 290–304.
Oh, S., & Lewis, C. (2008). Korean preschoolers' advanced inhibitory control and its relation to other executive skills and mental state understanding. *Child Development, 79,* 80–99.
Park, S.-Y., & Cheah, C.S.L. (2005). Korean mothers' proactive socialization beliefs regarding preschoolers' social skills. *International Journal of Behavioral Development, 29,* 24–34.
Parmar, P., Harkness, S., & Super, C. M. (2004). Asian and Euro-American parents' ethnotheories of play and learning: Effects on preschool children's home routines and school behavior. *International Journal of Behavioral Development, 28,* 97–104.
Perner, J. 1991. *Understanding the representational mind.* Cambridge, MA: MIT Press.
Perner, J., & Lang, B. (2000). Theory of mind and executive function: Is there a developmental relationship? In S. Baron-Cohen, H. Tager-Flusberg, & D. Cohen (Eds.), *Understanding other minds: Perspectives from autism and developmental cognitive neuroscience* (pp. 150–181). Oxford: Oxford University Press.
Perner, J., Lang, B., & Kloo, D. (2002). Theory of mind and self-control: More than a common problem of inhibition. *Child Development, 73,* 752–767.
Perner, J., Ruffman, T., & Leekam, S. R. (1994). Theory of mind is contagious: You catch it from your sibs. *Child Development, 65,* 1228–1238.
Peterson, C., & Slaughter, V. (2003). Opening windows into the mind: Mothers' preferences for mental state explanations and children's theory of mind. *Cognitive Development, 18,* 399–429.
Ruffman, T., Perner, J., Naito, M., Parkin, L., & Clements, W. A. (1998). Older (but not younger) siblings facilitate false belief understanding. *Developmental Psychology, 34,* 161–174.
Ruffman, T., Perner, J., & Parkin, L. (1999). How parenting style affects false belief understanding. *Social Development, 8,* 395–411.
Russell, J. (1996). *Agency: Its role in mental development.* Hove, England: Erlbaum Taylor & Francis.
Sabbagh, M., Xu, F., Carlson, S. M., Moses, L. J., & Lee, K. (2006). The development of executive functioning and theory of mind: A comparison of Chinese and U.S. preschoolers. *Psychological Science, 17,* 74–81.
Schneider, W., Schumann-Hengsteler, R., & Sodian, B. (Eds.), 2005. *Young children's cognitive development: Interrelationships among executive functioning, working memory, verbal ability, and theory of mind.* Mahwah, NJ: Erlbaum.
Short, B. (2007). *The effect of training and the transfer of skills between false belief, card sorting and inhibitory control tasks: Is one method of training superior?* M.Sc. dissertation, Department of Psychology, Lancaster University.
Taylor, J. (2005, February 8). China: One child policy. ABC News report. http://www.abc.net.au/foreign/content/2005/s1423772.htm
Tobin, J., Karasawa, M., & Hsueh, Y. (2004). Komatsudani then and now: Continuity and change in a Japanese preschool. *Contemporary Issues in Early Childhood, 5,* 128–144.

Tobin, J., Wu, D., & Davidson, D. (1989). *Preschool in three cultures: Japan, China and the United States.* New Haven, CT: Yale University Press.
Tomasello, M., Kruger, A. C., & Ratner, H. H. (1993). Cultural learning. *Behavioral and Brain Sciences, 16,* 495–552.
Vinden, P. (2001). Parenting attitudes and children's understanding of mind: A comparison of Korean American and Anglo-American families. *Cognitive Development, 16,* 793–809.
Wang, J., & Mao, S. 1996. Culture and the kindergarten curriculum in the People's Republic of China. *Early Child Development and Care, 123,* 143–156.
Wellman, H. M. (1990). *The child's theory of mind.* Cambridge, MA: MIT Press.
Wellman, H. M., Cross, D., & Watson, J. (2001). Meta-analysis of theory-of-mind development: The truth about false belief. *Child Development, 72,* 655–684.

CHARLIE LEWIS, *professor of family and developmental psychology at Lancaster University, conducts research on family relationships, especially the role of the father, and also young children's social cognitive development.*

MASUO KOYASU, *professor of developmental psychology in the Graduate School of Education in Kyoto University, has had a long-standing interest in research into perspective taking in young children, following Piaget's classic experiments.*

SEUNGMI OH *is a developmental psychologist who obtained her Ph.D. at Lancaster University by studying development of social understanding in children in Korea and is currently publishing her work on a range of social skills in early development.*

AYAKO OGAWA *is a doctoral candidate in developmental psychology in the Graduate School of Education in Kyoto University.*

BENJAMIN SHORT *obtained his B.Sc. and M.Sc. at Lancaster University and has recently shifted careers to become a management trainee.*

ZHAO HUANG *received her M.Sc. from Lancaster University.*

Carlson, S. M. (2009). Social origins of executive function development. In C. Lewis & J. I. M. Carpendale (Eds.), Social interaction and the development of executive function. New Directions in Child and Adolescent Development, 123, 87–97.

Social Origins of Executive Function Development

Stephanie M. Carlson

Abstract

The chapters in this issue revisit the social origins of the development of executive function (EF) through both empirical examination of the contexts in which EF development occurs (in vivo), as well as its social antecedents and consequences. Importantly, they also point to new directions in studying the social foundations of neurodevelopment, novel methods that take the social context into account, and cultural influences on EF development. © Wiley Periodicals, Inc.

The chapters in this issue revisit the social origins of the development of executive function (EF) with a new and important twist: empirical examination of the contexts in which EF development occurs (*in vivo*), as well as its social progenitors and consequences. Threads in EF research in the past decade have focused on atypical development (executive dysfunction, as in ADHD and autism), efforts toward establishing normative benchmarks (psychometrics), proposed psychological mechanisms and neural substrates, and the cognitive/academic and social correlates of individual differences in EF. Far less emphasis has been placed on the link between social interaction and EF, but as these chapters clearly illustrate the time is ripe for systematic investigation of both the proximal and distal social influences on neurocognitive development.

Modes and Motivations

This omission in past research is surprising given that there is a rich history of theoretical analysis on the very *social* origins of development of control over the self, by the self. As Lewis and Carpendale pointed out in the introduction to this issue, the Vygotsky-Luria tradition emphasized the role of social processes in executive attention and control skills. For Vygotsky (1978), development of EF flows out of social interaction by way of symbol systems (most prominently, language) that are the "tools" of society, and as these cultural tools become more semiotically sophisticated (as a function of sociopolitical geography or development) minds become less literal and reliant on the presence of concrete stimuli for thinking and reasoning about them. Indeed, it might not be an overstatement to claim, as Singer and Herman (1954) did, that "the ability to defer immediate motor response directed toward need gratification with the consequent resort to the realm of fantasy gives man a control of his future through imagery and planning . . . [and] may well be one of the key phases of maturation and, more broadly, civilization" (p. 330). In the Vygotskian view, though, it is worth noting that social interaction is a *vehicle* for transmission of the cultural tools of language and related symbol systems (such as pretense) that are engaged in the service of executive control. It is a social influence on EF with a degree of separation. Early developmental theorists articulated that self-control emerges via increasing reflection and deliberation among alternative possible responses, which requires distancing from reflexive, prepotent responses (Baldwin, 1892; Mead, 1910). In symbolic thought one is capable of responding in light of the symbol rather than the stimulus itself (that is, "psychological distancing"; Luria, 1961; Sigel, 1970, 1993).

Evidence from reverse contingency tasks supports this model. Apperly and Carroll (in press), using the Windows task (where children need to point to an empty box to receive a reward), and Carlson, Davis, and Leach (2005), using the Less Is More task (in which one needs to point to fewer candies in order to receive more), found that symbolic substitution (an elephant to represent a lot of candy and a mouse to represent a little) gave three-year-old children a means for working out the rule and inhibiting a prepotent response of pointing to the one they wanted for themselves. Most important, they sustained a high level of performance even when the more tempting stimulus (here, real candy) was introduced (Beck & Carlson, 2007). This appears *not* to be the case in chimpanzees, who were able to succeed on an analogous task with symbolic stimuli but immediately, and repeatedly, failed to inhibit when shown real treats (Boysen & Berntson, 1995). These findings suggest that symbols, which are often conventionally determined and socially transmitted, are a powerful tool for conscious control of the mind.

A different, and even more "social," link to EF concerns motivation: a direct reason for *wanting* to exert control over the self also likely has its origins in social interaction. Mead (1934) sketched a theory of how self-consciousness and control grow out of interaction with a caregiver. When the child acts on an impulse, it elicits a reaction from the caregiver, and this reaction (and similarly, many others) becomes internalized such that gradually the child automatically assumes "roles" (enacted in imaginative play) that are self-regulating. This self-regulation is important because it also helps regulate the *relationship* with the caregiver. Later attachment researchers acknowledged that children are likely to be motivated to attain self-control over their behavior at least in part so as not to jeopardize the attachment relationship (Sroufe, 1996).

As Lewis and Carpendale noted in the introduction to this issue, research examining development of self-regulation, particularly in delay-of-gratification situations, has placed a more central emphasis on child-caregiver relationships (for a review and meta-analysis, see Karreman, van Tuijl, van Aken, & Dekovi, 2006). This pertains to behavioral regulation of the type most likely to get adults' attention, such as resisting hitting a sibling and compliance with commands, but it also has consequences for the more purely cognitive aspects of EF, such as those engaged in academic problem solving. Having a mutually responsive and secure relationship with a caregiver is likely to make parental scaffolding more frequent, and more pleasurable and effective when it does occur.

Proximal and Distal Social Influences

These chapters supply evidence of both proximal and distal influences on development of EF, or "deliberate" and "incidental," to borrow from Hughes and Ensor's piece.

First, Bibok, Carpendale, and Müller take a microgenetic approach to examining the relation between scaffolding and EF (attention switching). They found strong support for the importance of timing and contingency in parental scaffolding behaviors (especially elaborative utterances) while children attempted a moderately challenging puzzle task. The authors noted that "parents therefore serve as an auxiliary and exogenous form of attention-switching EF for their children." The precision in this approach is laudable. It also speaks to the attachment link just described, in that the very earliest parent-child interactions, which might not yet qualify as having to do with "representation," nevertheless help establish expectancies about the pattern of social reciprocity at a temporal level (see Trevarthen & Aitken, 2001). Bibok et al. contend that cognition may be inherently interactive and temporal in nature, rather than representational (Bickhard & Terveen, 1995). Consider, however, imitation, which has been proposed as a likely beginning of self-other equivalence and shared intentionality (Baldwin, 1892; Baressi & Moore, 1996). Meltzoff and Moore (1994) showed that both structural and temporal synchrony appear to be necessary in infants' awareness of being imitated (you do *what* I do *when* I do it). In a similar vein, scaffolding might be more likely detected and effective if it is well timed and aimed at the child's current representational level of understanding the problem at hand.

Developmental timing, too, is an important consideration, because scaffolding might follow an inverted-U pattern in relation to child age and ability. Bibok et al. had as participants two-year-olds. In older children, with the same task, more scaffolding might be correlated with *lower* EF because the child's delayed EF is eliciting more parental scaffolding, or because the parent has a history of being inappropriately intrusive, thus not allowing for the internalization process and fostering the child's dependency on external sources of control. As Bibok et al. noted, it is a limitation that child-to-mother response contingencies were not scored. These would be needed to examine the child's role as a self-scaffolder. According to Bickhard's analysis (1992), the child plays an active role, and so it is likely to be a dynamic system between these two players. This hypothesis is consistent with findings by Landry and colleagues showing that parent directive utterances (which limit freedom of action in the task) were associated with positive outcomes at 2.5 years of age, but with poorer outcomes in children just one year older, who were presumably more autonomous and found the directives to be intrusive and out of sync (Landry, Smith, Swank, & Miller-Loncar, 2000). Note, however, that directives were not negatively related to EF in the Bibok et al. study; they were simply not related, whereas elaboratives were positively related to children's EF. Thus elaborative utterances might be the more promising measure of focus in studying specific scaffolding techniques facilitating EF at certain points in development.

Hughes and Ensor also examined maternal scaffolding but at a more generic level than Bibok et al., including the extent to which mothers engaged in open-ended questions, praise, encouragement, and elaborations during a structured activity. They also included a large set of moderately distal (family-level) variables to sort out the general cognitive and social-interactive influences on EF in children from age two to four years, including mothers' own modeling of EF, family chaos, and inconsistent parenting. Results indicated support for both proximal and distal influences on EF at age four, even after accounting for EF at age two and verbal ability. Most strikingly, the "general negative" variable of family chaos predicted a *lack* of normal and expected developmental change in EF, whereas "general positive" variables such as maternal calm responsiveness predicted continuity in EF rankings relative to other children in the sample over time. This highlights the potential of disorganized and unpredictable family environments to derail an otherwise normal progression of EF in a "good enough" caregiving environment (Scarr, 2000).

An interesting implication of Hughes and Ensor's work is that there is a great deal of unconscious parenting happening (for better or worse) when it comes to children's developing EF. It is perhaps a bit embarrassing for readers who are themselves parents to realize how unaware we are of the direct guidance we provide and, crucially, the indirect ways we transmit messages to children about self-regulation via modeling and family systems and organization, regardless of certain background factors such as SES.

Together, the papers on scaffolding set a context for understanding EF development within social interaction. They suggest that although deliberate efforts to regulate children's executive attention and problem solving show some specific benefits, the effects of social interaction on children's development cannot be reduced to the individual contributions of the participants. Investigators need to consider contingency and timing of the interactions, as well as what Hughes and Ensor refer to as "children's incidental exposure to family environments that can help or hinder goal-directed thought and action." In addition, given the surprisingly low correlation between family interaction variables and SES, this research suggests that using SES as a token measure of "environment" might be painting with too broad a brush. It is important to note, however, that Hughes and Ensor's disadvantaged sample might not have had sufficient variability in SES to reveal these associations with family chaos and inconsistency.

Landry, Smith, and Swank shift the focus from social interaction *influences* on EF as measured in the usual cognitive context to *social problem solving* itself, and what it reveals about children's developing self-control and social competence. They sought to capture integration of skills believed to contribute to successful social problem solving with a new measure appropriate for middle childhood. Their Monopoly teaching task can be thought of as a socially embedded theory-of-mind task, in which it is necessary to consider differing mental states, as well as a dyadic EF task. Here children themselves are doing the scaffolding that parents did in Bibok et al. and Hughes and Ensor's study. Landry et al. found that individual differences in performance on the Monopoly task were significantly correlated with verbal ability, attention, memory, and planning at age eight. Furthermore, peer collaboration and effective conflict discussion with a parent at age 13 were significantly predicted by the Monopoly task. What remains unclear, however, is how consistent these relations are if verbal ability is statistically controlled. Indeed, the variables identified as potential precursors to performance on the Monopoly task—social communication with parents and solitary pretend play with objects assessed at age three—were shown to be fully mediated by children's language skills assessed at age six. It is possible that socially oriented pretense (shared intentions, role play, and imaginary companions) might be a more sensitive measure in predicting later teaching ability (e.g., Taylor & Carlson, 1997). Even so, this is testimony to the fact that the teaching task taps into precisely the constellation of skills Landry et al. identified as important for social problem solving, including but not likely reducible to verbal intelligence.

Recent studies with preschool children support the notion of teaching as an activity that is closely associated with social understanding and EF, in keeping with the proposal by Tomasello, Kruger, and Ratner (1993). Davis-Unger and Carlson (2008b) adapted a task in which children first learn how to play a simple board game having eight rules (for example, players can move in only one direction) and then are asked to teach another (a confederate learner) how to play. Coding included the time spent teaching, number of rules taught, and the number of strategies employed in teaching. Children's teaching effectiveness improved dramatically from age 3.5 to 5.5 years and was significantly correlated with theory-of-mind performance (false belief tasks), even after controlling for age. This result suggests that, as Landry et al. proposed, teaching incorporates a social understanding of other minds and sensitive attempts to close the knowledge gap. A second, larger study ($N = 82$) took into account the executive control aspects of teaching as well. EF skills recruited in teaching are numerous. They include goal-directedness, planning, and working memory, as well as inhibition of the impulse to "just let me do it for you" and continuous monitoring of the learner's progress and flexible attempts to correct errors. Davis-Unger and Carlson (2008a) again found age-related improvement in teaching. More important, when examined separately both theory of mind and EF predicted performance on the teaching task, independent of age, verbal ability (Stanford-Binet Early 5), and memory capacity (digit span). When pitted against one another in a hierarchical multiple regression analysis, EF explained unique variance in teaching over and above theory of mind and the controls, whereas the reverse was not true when theory of mind was entered into the equation last.

There is a dearth of social problem-solving measures for early and middle childhood that tap into children's dyadic EF skills. These naturalistic and socially meaningful measures, such as examining children's teaching, will be important complements to the neuropsychological approach to understanding EF development as well as its social origins and sequelae.

Lewis, Koyasu, Oh, Ogawa, Short, and Huang examined cultural differences in the links between EF and social understanding, which might be considered the most distal influence in this set of chapters. As the authors acknowledged, culture is "a complete package" and often used as a proxy for ideological differences, values, and beliefs about the nature of children, as well as observable differences in daily life. Lewis et al. offer a very interesting comparison of four cultures (China, Japan, Korea, and the UK) to previous tests of the EF-ToM relation in Chinese preschoolers (Sabbagh, Xu,

Carlson, Moses, & Lee, 2006). The answer to their first question as to whether the relation between EF and ToM is universal in Western and Asian cultures was a resounding no. These inconsistent findings will need to be reconciled. One issue is whether there was less variance in the Asian samples than the UK sample. Even without the problem of ceiling effects, if the majority of the children's scores are falling into a small range then correlations will be affected. The magnitude of the task intercorrelations making up the composite scores might also play a role, with lower cohesion of the battery contributing more noise. With the exception of the Chinese sample, however, the pattern suggests that the bivariate correlations were similar across cultures, but more steeply attenuated after controlling for age and verbal ability in the Asian groups. Examination of the strength of the correlations with chronological and mental age would address this issue. Nonetheless, this impressive set of studies shows differences in the developmental pace of EF development (strikingly accelerated in Korea) as well as differences in the nature of its relations to social understanding and parenting variables. There are no answers yet, but this is a crucial first step in documenting these aspects of development cross-culturally.

As a complement to traditional cross-cultural investigations in which "culture" is treated as the independent variable, it is important to study the more specific ways culture is instantiated—in other words, to remember to connect the dots between the distal and proximal levels of analysis of social influences on EF. The examination by Lewis et al. of Chinese children living under the one-child policy is an example of this approach. Further investigation of how self-control and social understanding are fostered is needed. For example, is it possible that the preschool education practices in Korea inculcate a more rote, less reflective way of regulating responses that is not yet internalized, generalized, or sustained in the absence of caregivers or authority figures? It is also interesting to note that the general pattern of better EF performance in Asian children consistently fails to hold up for delay-of-gratification tasks, in which they perform similarly or even slightly worse than Western children (Carlson & Choi, 2008; Oh & Lewis, 2008; Sabbagh et al., 2006). Again, a closer look at cultural meaning is warranted. It could be that a history of limited resources makes it maladaptive to wait, that children are more indulged, that there is a "hurry-hurry" pace to daily life that makes waiting in these tasks seem ludicrous, or that the differences disappear in more emotional-motivational "hot" EF tasks.

Another example of looking at *how* cultural values are instantiated comes from Talwar, Carlson, and Lee's report (2008) of children's EF in schools with and without corporal punishment in West Africa. Indeed, this reflects an age-old debate spanning from John Locke (1693) and Jean Jacques Rousseau (1762) to current controversy in the academic and popular press over use of coercive punitive methods versus positive reinforcement and inductive discipline to achieve child compliance (e.g., Baumrind, 1996). Tasks included a "cool" (relatively nonaffective) and "hot" (relatively affective) version of three EF tasks: Delay of Gratification, Gift Delay, and Dimensional Change Card Sort. Children had more difficulty with the hot versions of the tasks than the cool versions, and older children outperformed younger children. A consistent pattern of interaction between school and grade level emerged. Kindergarten children in the punitive school performed significantly *better* than their counterparts in the nonpunitive school. This pattern was reversed for first grade children; those in the punitive school performed significantly *worse* than their counterparts in the nonpunitive school. These findings suggest that a harsh punitive environment may have short-term gains but long-term detrimental effects on children's EF. This research points to the need to consider interactions among discipline style, age, and internalization processes of self-regulation in order to better understand environmental influences on EF development.

New Directions

These papers mark a return to serious consideration of the social origins of EF. Followers of this approach will likely focus on the neuroscience and measurement of EF in more social terms.

First, growing interest has emerged for the hypothesis that early relational experiences are closely related to child neurocognitive development. The compelling link between quality of parent-child relationships and child cognitive development is often presumed to be due to the interplay between genetic factors and the social environment in shaping early brain development (De Bellis, 2001; Schore, 1996). According to Glaser (2000), orderly development of the frontal lobes, strongly implicated in EF, is dependent on "appropriate input and sensitive interaction with the primary caregivers" (p. 101). Given that prefrontal cortex is a slow-developing area, with neural density of the frontal lobes beginning to decline at only about seven years of age (Huttenlocher, 2002), there is indeed a large window of plasticity during which caregiving can have a significant impact on the developing structures. Although animal studies have documented the impact of parental care on development of prefrontal systems (Gunnar et al., 2006), human research is limited, pertaining mostly to highly inadequate caregiving.

To partly address this gap, Bernier, Carlson, and Whipple (in press) conducted a prospective longitudinal study to investigate links between quality of parent-infant interactions and subsequent EF, including working memory, impulse control, and set shifting. Maternal sensitivity, mind-mindedness and autonomy-support were assessed when children were 12 to 15 months old ($N = 80$). Child EF was assessed at 18 and 26 months of age. Results revealed that all three parenting dimensions were related to child EF. However, consistent with Hughes and Ensor's results presented here, autonomy-support (which included scaffolding during a moderately difficult puzzle task) as well as mind-mindedness made unique contributions to later EF, independent of general cognitive ability and maternal education. These findings reinforce previous results on child stress-response systems in suggesting that parent-child relationships may be an important mechanism underlying development of children's self-regulatory capacities.

Second, more direct comparisons of EF measures in social and relatively nonsocial scenarios will shed light on this topic with greater experimental control than large-scale correlation studies can achieve. For example, Prencipe and Zelazo (2005) reported that three-year-olds were significantly better at affective decision making (choosing to forgo a smaller reward now for a larger reward later) when making choices for the experimenter rather than for themselves. The authors argued that prior to integrating the perspectives of self and other, children are able to work out the best option for someone else, but one's own desire gets in the way and leads to failure to inhibit when it comes to making decisions for the self (Barresi & Moore, 1996). A corollary is that children might first learn to appreciate what an alternative response would be by thinking about *someone else* making it.

Similarly, *observing* someone else make correct responses in an executive control task is another avenue toward success. For example, Moriguchi, Lee, and Itakura (2007) applied a social learning model to the Dimensional Change Card Sort task (Zelazo, 2006) and found that preschool children were much less likely to imitate a model who was sorting incorrectly if the model expressed doubt than if she expressed confidence or obliviousness to her errors. These results suggest that social learning mechanisms of observation, reinforcement, and imitation of models should be considered in addition to the more theoretically steeped but abstract theories of internalization and psychological distancing mentioned earlier. Indeed, social learning contributes to formation of dominance hierarchies even in preschool classrooms, which strongly encourage regulation of the self if only for fear of being ostracized (Pellegrini et al., 2007).

Lastly, distal, often vague, and unwieldy cultural influences on EF development will be brought down to size via more quasi-experimental studies. The approach by Talwar et al. (2008) of comparing subsets of a given culture that differ on factors believed to be contributing to EF development (in this case, inductive discipline) is one example. Another possibility is to activate culturally based values around self-control via "culture priming" with bicultural children (e.g., displaying cultural icons during testing), a technique that has been employed recently in behavioral and imaging studies in adult social psychology (e.g., Kemmelmeier & Cheng, 2004).

In summary, the studies presented in this issue and these examples of new directions are meant to bring together a renewed emphasis on social interaction links to EF with the traditional focus on its neurological bases in ways that could be very fruitful for understanding of the emergence of EF in individuals-in-context.

References

Apperly, I., & Carroll, D. (in press). How do symbols affect 3-year-olds' executive function? Evidence from a reverse-contingency task. *Developmental Science.*

Baldwin, J. M. (1892). Origin of volition in childhood. *Science, 20,* 286–287.

Barresi, J., & Moore, C. (1996). Intentional relations and social understanding. *Behavioral and Brain Sciences, 19,* 107–154.

Baumrind, D. (1996). A blanket injunction against disciplinary use of spanking is not warranted by the data. *Pediatrics, 98,* 828–831.

Beck, D. M., & Carlson, S. M. (2007, June). *Symbolic transfer in the "less is more" measure of executive function.* Poster presented at the annual meeting of the Jean Piaget Society, Amsterdam, Netherlands.

Bernier, A., Carlson, S. M., & Whipple, N. (in press). From external regulation to self-regulation: Early parenting precursors of young children's executive functioning. *Child Development.*

Bickhard, M. H. (1992). Scaffolding and self-scaffolding: Central aspects of development. In L. T Winegar & J. Valsiner (Eds.), *Children's development within social context: Vol. 1. Metatheory and theory* (pp. 33–52). Mahwah, NJ: Erlbaum.

Bickhard, M. H., & Terveen, L. (1995). *Foundational issues in artificial intelligence and cognitive science: Impasse and solution.* Amsterdam, Netherlands: Elsevier.

Boysen, S. T., & Berntson, G. G. (1995). Responses to quantity: Perceptual versus cognitive mechanisms in chimpanzees (*Pan troglodytes*). *Journal of Experimental Psychology, 21,* 82–86.

Carlson, S. M., & Choi, H. P. (2008, July). Bilingualism and cultural influences on the development of executive function. In L. Wijnroks (Chair), *The development of executive attention and cognitive control in infancy and early childhood: Influence of experience and biological risk.* Paper symposium presented at the biennial meeting of the International Society for the Study of Behavioral Development, Würzburg, Germany.

Carlson, S. M., Davis, A., & Leach, J. G. (2005). Less is more: Executive function and symbolic representation in preschool children. *Psychological Science, 16,* 609–616.

Davis-Unger, A. C., & Carlson, S. M. (2008a). Children's teaching: Relations to theory of mind and executive function. *Mind, Brain, and Education, 2,* 128–135.

Davis-Unger, A. C., & Carlson, S. M. (2008b). Development of teaching ability in preschool children and relations to theory of mind. *Journal of Cognition and Development, 9,* 26–45.

De Bellis, M. D. (2001). Developmental traumatology: The psychobiological development of maltreated children and implication for research, treatment and policy. *Development and Psychopathology, 13,* 539–564.

Glaser, D. (2000). Child abuse and neglect and the brain: A review. *Journal of Child Psychology and Psychiatry, 41,* 97–116.

Gunnar, M. R., & the Early Experience, Stress and Prevention Network (2006). Bringing basic research on early experience and stress neurobiology to bear on preventive interventions for neglected and maltreated children. *Development and Psychopathology, 18,* 651–677.

Huttenlocher, P. R. (2002). *Neural plasticity: The effects of environment on the development of the cerebral cortex.* Cambridge, MA: Harvard University Press.

Karreman, A., van Tuijl, C., van Aken, M.A.G., & Dekovi, M. (2006). Parenting and self-regulation: A meta-analysis. *Infant and Child Development, 15,* 561–579.

Kemmelmeier, M., & Cheng, B. Y. (2004). Language and self-construal priming: A replication and extension in a Hong Kong sample. *Journal of Cross-Cultural Psychology, 35,* 705–712.

Landry, S. H., Smith, K. E., Swank, P. R., & Miller-Loncar, C. L. (2000). Early maternal and child influences on children's later independent cognitive and social functioning. *Child Development, 71,* 358–375.

Locke, J. (1693/1909–14). *Some thoughts concerning education.* Harvard Classics (vol. 37). New York: P. F. Collier & Son.

Luria, A. R. (1961). *The role of speech in the regulation of normal and abnormal behavior.* Oxford: Pergamon.

Mead, G. H. (1910). What objects must psychology presuppose? *Journal of Philosophy, Psychology, and Scientific Methods, 7,* 174–180.

Mead, G. H. (1934). *Mind, self, and society from the standpoint of a social behaviorist.* Chicago: University of Chicago Press.

Meltzoff, A. N., & Moore, M. K. (1994). Imitation, memory, and the representation of persons. *Infant Behavior and Development, 17,* 83–99.

Moriguchi, Y., Lee, K., & Itakura, S. (2007). Social transmission of disinhibition in young children. *Developmental Science, 10,* 481–491.

Oh, S., & Lewis, C. (2008). Korean preschoolers' advanced inhibitory control and its relation to other executive skills and mental state understanding. *Child Development, 79,* 80–99.

Pellegrini, A. D., et al. (2007). Social dominance in preschool classrooms. *Journal of Comparative Psychology, 121,* 54–64.

Prencipe, A., & Zelazo, P. D. (2005). Development of affective decision making for self and other: Evidence for the integration of first- and third-person perspectives. *Psychological Science, 16,* 501–505.

Rousseau, J. J. (1762/1979). *Emile, or On Education.* Trans. Allan Bloom. New York: Basic Books.

Sabbagh, M. A., Xu, F., Carlson, S. M., Moses, L. J., & Lee, K. (2006). The development of executive functioning and theory of mind: A comparison of Chinese and U.S. preschoolers. *Psychological Science, 17,* 74–81.

Scarr, S. (2000). American childcare today. In A. Slater & D. Muir (Eds.), *Blackwell Reader in Developmental Psychology.* Oxford, England: Blackwell.

Schore, A. N. (1996). The experience-dependant maturation of a regulatory system in the orbital prefrontal cortex and the origin of developmental psychopathology. *Development and Psychopathology, 8,* 59–87.

Sigel, I. E. (1970). The distancing hypothesis: A causal hypothesis for the acquisition of representational thought. In M. R. Jones (Ed.), *Miami Symposium on the Prediction of Behavior, 1968: Effects of early experience* (pp. 99–118). Coral Gables, FL: University of Miami Press.

Sigel, I. E. (1993). The centrality of a distancing model for the development of representational competence. In R. R. Cocking & K. A. Renninger (Eds.), *The development and meaning of psychological distance* (pp. 141–157). Hillsdale, NJ: Erlbaum.

Singer, J. L., & Herman, J. (1954). Motor and fantasy correlates of Rorschach human movement responses. *Journal of Consulting Psychology, 18,* 325–331.

Sroufe, L. A. (1996). *Emotional development: The organization of emotional life in the early years.* Cambridge: Cambridge University Press.

Talwar, V., Carlson, S. M., & Lee, K. (2008). Effects of a punitive environment on children's executive functioning: A natural experiment. Manuscript under review.

Taylor, M., & Carlson, S. M. (1997). The relation between individual differences in fantasy and theory of mind. *Child Development, 68,* 436–455.

Tomasello, M., Kruger, A. C., & Ratner, H. H. (1993). Cultural learning. *Behavioral and Brain Sciences, 16,* 495–552.

Trevarthen, C., & Aitken, K. J. (2001). Infant intersubjectivity: Research, theory, and clinical applications. *Journal of Child Psychology & Psychiatry 42,* 3–48.
Vygotsky, L. S. (1978). *Mind in Society.* Cambridge, MA: Harvard University Press.
Zelazo, P. D. (2006). The Dimensional Change Card Sort (DCCS): A method of assessing executive function in children. *Nature Protocols, 1,* 297–301.

STEPHANIE M. CARLSON *is associate professor in the Institute of Child Development, University of Minnesota, Minneapolis.*

INDEX

Aadmodt-Leeper, G., 7
Achenbach, T. M., 54
Acker, M., 41
Aitken, K. J., 90
Altshuler, J., 63
Anderson, S. J., 61
Andrich, D., 56
Apperly, I., 88
Ardila, A., 5
Arnold, D., 41
Aron, A. R., 5
Asbury, K., 37
Assel, M. A., 62
Astington, J. W., 52, 70
Attentional flexibility, 2, 6, 7
Atzaba-Poria, N., 39

Baddeley, A. D., 2
Baird, J. A., 70
Bakeman, R., 27
Baker, N., 4
Baldwin, J. M., 88, 90
Baressi, J., 90, 95
Barnes, C., 36
Baumrind, D., 73, 93
Beck, D. M., 89
Beeghly, M., 26
Bernier, A., 94
Berntson, G. G., 89
Berridge, D., 72
Bibok, M. B., 11, 17, 34, 36, 38, 89, 90, 91
Bickhard, M. H., 22, 27, 31, 32, 90
Bishop, D. V. M., 7
Bowerman, M., 81
Boysen, S. T., 89
Brace, J. J., 9
Bradley, R., 37
Bretherton, I., 26, 62
Breton, C., 71
British Picture Vocabulary Scale, 42
Broadbent, D. E., 2
Bruner, J. S., 18, 23, 27, 62
Bull, R., 7
Burke, S., 36

Cameron, C., 38
Campbell, R. L., 22

Carlson, S., 10, 11, 12, 26, 52, 70, 71, 72, 87, 88, 89, 92, 93, 94, 97
Carpendale, J. I. M., 1, 6, 11, 15, 17, 24, 25, 34, 36, 38, 69, 70, 72, 88, 89
Carroll, D., 88
Chandler, M. J., 73
Chang, F.-M., 81
Chao, R., 71
Chapieski, M. L., 54
Chasiotis, A., 73
Cheah, C. S. L., 81
Cheng, B. Y., 95
Choi, H. P., 93
Choi, S., 81
Clements, 72
Cognitive Complexity and Control (CCC) theory, 8
Coldwell, J., 41
Cole, K., 72
Collins, W. A., 61
Confucius, 82
Conger, A. J., 28
Conger, R. D., 61
Connor, C., 38
Corley, R. P., 6
Corwyn, R., 37
Cox, J. L., 26
Coy, K. C., 61
Crawford, A., 61
Cresswell, C., 7
Cross, D., 70
Cruess, L., 8
Cultural processes and social and executive skills, 11–12, 69–82
Cutting, A. L., 72

Dahl, R., 53
Dale, P. S., 26, 40
Davidson, D., 70
Davis, 88
Davis, A. C., 10
Davis, H. L., 75
Davis-Unger, A. C., 92
Day-Night test, 5, 7, 8, 74, 75, 76
De Bellis, M. D., 94
Deater-Deckard, K., 41, 47
DeFries, J. C., 6
Dekovi, M., 5, 89

Delay of gratification, 4–5
Derryberry, D., 5
deVilliers, J. G., 52
Diamond, A., 5, 7, 8
Diggle, P., 7
Dimensional Change Card Sort (DCCS), 8–9, 72, 74, 75, 77, 93, 95
Dodge, K., 47
Dolan, C. V., 7
Donaldson, M., 55
Drinkwater, M., 61
Duncan, J., 7, 36
Dunn, J., 37, 39, 41, 42, 52, 72

Edelstein, W., 59
Eisenberg, N., 52
Elder, G., 61
Elkins, I., 61
Elliott, C., 42
Emerson, M. J., 6
Emmons, B. A., 4
Emslie, H., 7
Ensor, R. A., 11, 21, 27, 35, 38, 42, 50, 89, 90, 91, 94
Eslinger, P., 36
Espy, K. A., 7, 54
Executive function: cultural processes and, 69–82; families and emergence of, 35–48; parental scaffolding and, 17–33; social interaction and, 1–12; social origins of, 87–95; social problem solving and, 51–65

Fabes, R. A., 52
False belief tasks, defined, 70
Families and emergence of executive function, 35–48. *See also* Parental scaffolding and development of executive function
Fang, F., 59
Fang, G., 59
Farah, M. J., 5, 38
Farris, C., 38
Farver, J. A. M., 73
Feldman, R., 62
Fenson, L., 26, 62
Fernyhough, C., 6
Flavell, J. H., 4
Fleiss, J. L., 56
Flynn, E., 72
Freedman, D. J., 36
Freeman, N., 72
Freer, C., 8

French, L., 71, 73
Freud, S., 2
Freund, L. S., 27, 32
Frick, T., 56, 60, 61
Friedman, N. P., 6
Frye, D., 5, 8, 71, 72
Fuerst, D. R., 52
Fuligni, A., 61

Garcia-Villamisar, D., 37
Gardner, F., 41
Garfield, J., 64
Gatz, M., 37
Gerstadt, C. L., 5, 7
Gioia, G. A., 54
Glaser, D., 94
Global negative model, 39, 41
Global positive model, 38, 41
Glover, G., 36
Golden, C., 36
Gottman, J. M., 27
Graham, A., 36
Grayson, A., 36
Greenblatt, E., 54
Guajardo, S., 5
Gunnar, M. R., 94
Gur, R. C., 37
Gur, R. E., 37
Guthrie, I. K., 52
Guttentag, C., 60

Hagen, E. P., 43, 57
Hala, S., 10, 71, 72
Hall, S., 54
Halperin, J. M., 57
Harkness, S., 73
Harlan, E. T., 21, 26, 28
Haworth, C., 40
Heaton, S., 40
Hebert-Myers, H., 60
Henderson, A., 71
Hendriks-Jansen, H., 32
Herman, J., 88
Hess, R. D., 19, 20, 28
Hewitt, J. K., 6
Hitch, G. J., 2
Hix, H. R., 72
Hofer, F., 73
Hong, Y. J., 5, 7
Howerter, A., 6
Hsueh, Y., 70
Huang, Z., 69, 78, 85, 92
Hug, S., 71

Hughes, C. H., 10, 11, 21, 27, 35, 36, 37, 38, 42, 43, 50, 52, 71, 72, 89, 90, 91, 94
Huizinga, M., 7
Huttenlocher, P. R., 94

Iacono, W. G., 61
Imbens-Bailey, A. L., 63
Imitation model, 39, 41
Inhibitory control, 2, 6, 7
Internal States Language Questionnaire (ISLQ), 26
Isquith, P. K., 54
Itakura, S., 9, 95

Jacques, S., 6, 9
James, W., 3
Jenkins, J. M., 52
Jewkes, A., 38
Johnson, R., 8
Juujarvi, P., 7

Kaciroti, N., 11
Kagan, J., 62
Karasawa, M., 70
Karreman, A., 5, 89
Kearsley, R. B., 62
Keating, D., 53
Keller, M., 59
Kemmelmeier, M., 95
Kidd, J. R., 81
Kidd, K. K., 81
Kiessling, F., 73
Kim, J. K., 61
Kirkham, N. Z., 8, 9
Klein, P. S., 62
Kloo, D., 37, 72, 81
Knight, R. K., 5
Knowles, M., 7
Kobayashi, C., 36
Kochanska, G., 21, 26, 28, 62
Kooistra, L., 7
Kopp, C., 5
Kovas, Y., 40, 46
Koyama, K., 77
Koyasu, M., 11, 69, 85, 92
Kruger, A. C., 52, 70, 92
Kuczynski, L., 62
Kuntsi, J., 36
Kupfer, D. J., 53
Kurtz, M., 37
Kwon, Y.-I., 71, 73
Kyriakidou, C., 72

Lalonde, C. E., 73
Landry, S. H., 6, 11, 19, 20, 21, 23, 28, 31, 32, 51, 53, 54, 60, 62, 63, 68, 90, 91, 92
Lang, B., 71, 72
Laursen, B., 61
Leach, J. G., 10, 88
Lee, K., 9, 11, 70, 92, 93, 95
Leekam, S., 72
Lee-Shin, Y., 73
Lehto, J. E., 7
Lemery-Chalfant, K., 38
Levin, H. S., 57
Lewis, C., 1, 6, 7, 11, 12, 15, 69, 70, 71, 72, 78, 79, 85, 88, 89, 92, 93
Lezak, M. D., 52
Linacre, J. M., 56
Livak, K. J., 81
Locke, J., 93
Loeber, R., 61
Lorenz, F. O., 61
Ludwig, J., 41
Luft, I., 22
Luria, A. R., 3, 4, 6, 9, 38, 74, 88

Maccoby, E. E., 73
Mandell, D., 26
Mao, S., 71
Marcovitch, S., 5
Maridaki-Kassotaki, K., 6, 72
Martin, J. A., 73
Masten, A. S., 53
Matheny, A., 41
Matute, E., 5
Mauthner, N., 10
McCandliss, B. D., 5, 38
McClelland, M., 38
McCune-Nicolich, L., 63
McDevitt, T. M., 19, 20, 28
McGue, M., 61
McGurk, R., 7
Mead, G. H., 3, 12, 88, 89
Meiping, W., 61
Meltzoff, A. N., 90
Middle school social competence, predictors of, 63–64
Miller, E. K., 36
Miller, S. A., 4
Miller-Loncar, C. L., 19, 20, 54, 63, 90
Mischel, W., 4
Mitchell, P., 72
Miyake, A., 6
Moberg, P., 37

Monopoly social problem-solving task, 55–56, 57, 58, 62, 64, 65, 91
Moore, C., 90, 95
Moore, L. P., 4
Moore, M. K., 90
Moriguchi, Y., 9, 95
Morrison, F., 38
Morton, B. J., 9
Moses, L. J., 11, 52, 70, 71, 72, 92
Müller, U., 5, 6, 7, 11, 17, 34, 36, 38, 89
Munakata, Y., 8, 9
Murray, D., 42
Murray, K. T., 21, 26, 28, 62

Naito, M., 72, 77
Newton, E. L., 22
Noble, K. G., 5, 37, 44

Ogawa, A., 11, 69, 85, 92
Oh, S., 11, 69, 71, 74, 75, 85, 92, 93
O'Leary, S., 41
O'Malley, C., 72
Oriental children, executive skills in, 11, 69–82
Ozonoff, S., 36

Pakastis, A. J., 81
Palfai, T., 8, 71
Palmer, J., 54
Parental scaffolding and development of executive function, 11, 17–33
Parents, problem solving with, 61
Park, S.-Y., 81
Parkin, L., 70, 72
Parmar, P., 73
Patterson, C. J., 4
Pearson, L., 42
Peers, problem solving with, 59–61
Pellegrini, A. D., 95
Pelletier, J., 52
Pennington, B. F., 36, 52
Perner, J., 37, 70, 72, 81
Perry, T., 64
Peterson, C., 64, 72
Pethick, S., 26
Petrill, S., 41
Phillips, K., 41
Piaget, J., 31, 62
Pike, A., 37, 39, 41
Pine, D., 53
Play skills, role of early, 62–63
Plomin, R., 37, 40
Poggio, T., 36
Prencipe, A., 95

Problem solving, social, 11, 51–65
Pulkkinen, L., 7
Pyers, J. E., 52
Pylas, M., 41

Rabbitt, P., 7
Raizsner, R. D., 57
Rasch scaling, 55, 56, 58, 59, 65
Ratner, H. H., 52, 70, 92
Ray, L. S., 22
Reiser, M., 38, 52
Renda, C., 26
Renninger, K. A., 22
Rescorla, L. A., 54
Reuter, M. A., 61
Reznick, J. S., 26
Richardson, M. A., 54
Riesenhuber, M., 36
Ritchie, F. K., 4
Ronald, A., 36
Rooksby, M., 78
Roselli, M., 5
Ross, G., 18, 23, 27
Rothbart, M., 5
Rourke, B. P., 52
Rousseau, J. J., 93
Ruffman, T., 70, 72, 73, 79, 80
Russell, J., 10, 43
Rygh, J., 63

Sabbagh, M., 11, 70, 72, 73, 77, 81, 92, 93
Satish, U., 36
Sattler, J. M., 43, 57
Sayal, K., 41
Scaffolding: defined, 18–19; parental, 17–33; social structure of, 11
Scarr, S., 40, 91
Schmid, C., 59
Schmid-Schönbein, C., 24, 25
Schmidt, L. C., 61
Schneider, W., 70
Schore, A. N., 94
Schumann-Hengsteler, R., 70
Schwartz, S. T., 54
Secord, W., 63
Self-control in Korean culture, 73–74
Semcesen, T. K., 9
Semel, E., 63
Semmel, M., 56, 60, 61
Senn, T. E., 7
Shallice, T., 43, 54, 57
Sharma, V., 54
Sharpe, S., 10

Shelton, J., 4
Shimmon, K., 7
Short, B., 11, 69, 72, 85, 92
Sibling effect, 72
Sigel, I. E., 88
Singer, J. L., 88
Six Things task, 40, 41
Skuse, D., 7
Slaughter, V., 72
Slomkowski, C., 52
Smith, K. E., 6, 19, 20, 51, 53, 54, 60, 62, 63, 68, 90, 91
Smith, R., 2, 3, 4, 12
Snow, C. E., 63
So, C. W-C., 11
Social interaction and executive function, 1–12
Social origins of executive function development, 87–95
Social problem solving, 11, 51–65
Sodian, B., 70
Sokol, B. W., 6
Solis-Trapala, I., 7
Song, J., 57
Song, M., 71, 73
Sonuga-Barke, E., 41
Sroufe, L. A., 89
Steinberg, L., 53, 59
Streufert, S., 36
Stuss, D. T., 5
Subbotsky, E. V., 9
Super, C. M., 73
Swank, P. R., 11, 19, 20, 51, 53, 54, 60, 62, 63, 68, 90, 91

Talwar, V., 93, 95
Tardif, T., 11
Taylor, J., 80
Taylor, M., 92
Temple, E., 36
Terveen, L., 31
Test of Everyday Attention for Children, 40
Thorndike, R. L., 43, 57
Tidswell, T., 10

Tobin, J., 70, 81
Tomasello, M., 52, 70, 92
Toner, I., 4
Tower of London task, 43, 54, 57
Towse, J., 6, 7, 8, 9
Trevarthen, C., 90
Tseng, V., 71
Tulkin, S., 81

Valiente, C., 38, 39
van Aken, M. A. G., 5, 89
van der Molen, M. W., 7
van Tuijl, C., 5, 89
Velicer, W. F., 28
Vellet, S., 62
Vinden, P., 73
Vygotsky, L. S., 3, 4, 6, 8, 9, 38, 88

Wachs, T., 37, 41
Wager, T. D., 6
Walden, B., 61
Wang, J., 71
Watson, J., 70
Wellman, H. M., 70
Welsch, M. C., 52
Wenxin, Z., 61
Whipple, N., 94
Wiig, E. H., 63
Williams, L., 26
Williams, P., 8
Winter, V., 73
Witzki, A. H., 6
Wolf, D. P., 63
Wolff, L., 41
Wood, D., 11, 18, 22, 23, 27, 30, 72
Working memory, 2, 6, 7
Wu, D., 70

Xu, F, 11, 70, 92

Yerys, B. E., 8
Yin, Y., 61
Young, S. E., 6

Zelazo, P. D., 5, 6, 7, 8, 9, 62, 71, 95

OTHER TITLES AVAILABLE IN THE
NEW DIRECTIONS FOR CHILD AND ADOLESCENT DEVELOPMENT SERIES
Reed W. Larson and Lene Arnett Jensen, Editors-in-Chief
William Damon, Founding Editor-in-Chief

For a complete list of back issues, please visit www.josseybass.com/go/ndcad

CAD 122 **Core Competencies to Prevent Problem Behaviors and Promote Positive Youth Development**
Nancy G. Guerra, Catherine P. Bradshaw, Editors
Adolescence generally is considered a time of experimentation and increased involvement in risk or problem behaviors, including early school leaving, violence, substance use, and high-risk sexual behavior. In this volume, the authors show how individual competencies linked to well-being can reduce youth involvement in these risk behaviors. Five core competencies are emphasized: a positive sense of self, self-control, decision-making skills, a moral system of belief, and prosocial connectedness. A central premise of this volume is that high levels of the core competencies provide a marker for positive youth development, whereas low levels increase the likelihood of adolescent risk behavior. The authors summarize the empirical literature linking these competencies to each risk behavior, providing examples from developmental and prevention research. They highlight programs and policies in the United States and internationally that have changed one or more dimensions of the core competencies through efforts designed to build individual skills, strengthen relationships, and enhance opportunities and supports across multiple developmental contexts.
ISBN 978-04704-42166

CAD 121 **Beyond the Family: Contexts of Immigrant Children's Development**
Hirokazu Yoshikawa, Niobe Way, Editors
Immigration in the United States has become a central focus of policy and public concern in the first decade of the 21st century. This volume aims to broaden developmental research on children and youth in immigrant families. Much of the research on immigrant children and youth concentrates on family characteristics such as parenting, demographic, or human capital features. In this volume, we consider the developmental consequences for immigrant youth of broader contexts such as social networks, peer discrimination in school and out-of-school settings, legal contexts, and access to institutional resources. Chapters answer questions such as: How do experiences of discrimination affect the lives of immigrant youth? How do social networks of immigrant families influence children's learning? How do immigrant parents' citizenship status influence family life and their children's development? In examining factors as disparate as discrimination based on physical appearance, informal adult helpers, and access to drivers' licenses, these chapters serve to enrich our notions of how culture and context shape human development, as well as inform practice and public policy affecting immigrant families.
ISBN 978-04704-17300

CAD 120 **The Intersections of Personal and Social Identities**
Margarita Azmitia, Moin Syed, Kimberley Radmacher, Editors
This volume brings together an interdisciplinary set of social scientists who are pioneering ways to research and theorize the connections between personal and social identity development in children, adolescents, and emerging adults. The authors of the seven chapters address the volume's three goals: (1) illustrating how theory and research in identity develop-ment are enriched by an interdisciplinary approach, (2) providing a rich developmental picture of personal and social identity development, and (3) examining the connections among multiple identities. Several chapters provide practical suggestions for individuals, agencies, and schools and universities that work with children, adolescents, and emerging adults in diverse communities across the United States.
ISBN 978-04703-72838

CAD 119 **Social Class and Transitions to Adulthood**
Jeylan T. Mortimer, Editor
This volume of *New Directions for Child and Adolescent Development* is inspired by a stirring address that Frank Furstenberg delivered at the 2006 Meeting of the Society for Research on Adolescence, "Diverging Development: The Not So Invisible Hand of Social Class in the United States." He called on social scientists interested in the study of development to expand their purview beyond investigations of the developmental impacts of poverty and consider the full gamut of social class variation in our increasingly unequal society. The gradations of class alter the social supports, resources, and opportunities, as well as the constraints, facing parents as they attempt to guide their children toward the acquisition of adult roles. This volume examines the impacts of social class origin on the highly formative period of transition to adulthood. Drawing on findings from the Youth Development Study and other sources, the authors examine social class differences in adult child–parent relationships, intimacy and family formation, attainment of higher education, the school-to-work transition, the emergence of work-family conflict, and harassment in the workplace. The authors indicate new directions for research that will contribute to understanding the problems facing young people today. These chapters will persuade those making social policy to develop social interventions that will level the playing field and increase the opportunities for disadvantaged youth to become healthy and productive adults.
ISBN 978-04702-93621

CAD 118 **Social Network Analysis and Children's Peer Relationships**
Philip C. Rodkin, Laura D. Hanish, Editors
Social network analysis makes it possible to determine how large and dense children's peer networks are, how central children are within their networks, the various structural configurations that characterize social groups, and which peers make up individual children's networks. By centering the child within his or her social system, it is possible to understand the socialization processes that draw children toward or away from particular peers, as well as those who contribute to peer influence. This volume of *New Directions for Child and Adolescent Development* demonstrates how social network analysis provides insights into the ways in which peer groups contribute to children's and adolescents' development—from gender and intergroup relations, to aggression and bullying, to academic achievement. Together the chapters in this volume depict the complex, nested, and dynamic structure of peer groups and explain how social structure defines developmental processes.
ISBN 978-04702-59665

NEW DIRECTIONS FOR CHILD & ADOLESCENT DEVELOPMENT
ORDER FORM SUBSCRIPTION AND SINGLE ISSUES

DISCOUNTED BACK ISSUES:

Use this form to receive 20% off all back issues of *New Directions for Child & Adolescent Development*.
All single issues priced at **$23.20** (normally $29.00)

TITLE	ISSUE NO.	ISBN
_____	_____	_____
_____	_____	_____
_____	_____	_____

Call 888-378-2537 or see mailing instructions below. When calling, mention the promotional code JB9ND to receive your discount. For a complete list of issues, please visit www.josseybass.com/go/ndcad

SUBSCRIPTIONS: (1 YEAR, 4 ISSUES)

☐ New Order   ☐ Renewal

U.S.	☐ Individual: $85	☐ Institutional: $280
Canada/Mexico	☐ Individual: $85	☐ Institutional: $320
All Others	☐ Individual: $109	☐ Institutional: $354

Call 888-378-2537 or see mailing and pricing instructions below.
Online subscriptions are available at www.interscience.wiley.com

ORDER TOTALS:

Issue / Subscription Amount: $ _____
Shipping Amount: $ _____
(for single issues only – subscription prices include shipping)
Total Amount: $ _____

SHIPPING CHARGES:		
SURFACE	DOMESTIC	CANADIAN
First Item	$5.00	$6.00
Each Add'l Item	$3.00	$1.50

(No sales tax for U.S. subscriptions. Canadian residents, add GST for subscription orders. Individual rate subscriptions must be paid by personal check or credit card. Individual rate subscriptions may not be resold as library copies.)

BILLING & SHIPPING INFORMATION:

☐ **PAYMENT ENCLOSED:** *(U.S. check or money order only. All payments must be in U.S. dollars.)*
☐ **CREDIT CARD:**   ☐ VISA   ☐ MC   ☐ AMEX

Card number _____ Exp. Date _____
Card Holder Name _____ Card Issue # _____
Signature _____ Day Phone _____

☐ **BILL ME:** *(U.S. institutional orders only. Purchase order required.)*

Purchase order # _____
Federal Tax ID 13559302 • GST 89102-8052

Name _____
Address _____
Phone _____ E-mail _____

Copy or detach page and send to: **John Wiley & Sons, PTSC, 5th Floor**
989 Market Street, San Francisco, CA 94103-1741
Order Form can also be faxed to: **888-481-2665**

PROMO JB9ND

NEW DIRECTIONS FOR CHILD AND ADOLESCENT DEVELOPMENT IS NOW AVAILABLE ONLINE AT WILEY INTERSCIENCE

What is Wiley InterScience?

Wiley InterScience is the dynamic online content service from John Wiley & Sons delivering the full text of over 300 leading scientific, technical, medical, and professional journals, plus major reference works, the acclaimed Current Protocols laboratory manuals, and even the full text of select Wiley print books online.

What are some special features of Wiley InterScience?

Wiley Interscience Alerts is a service that delivers table of contents via e-mail for any journal available on Wiley InterScience as soon as a new issue is published online.

EarlyView is Wiley's exclusive service presenting individual articles online as soon as they are ready, even before the release of the compiled print issue. These articles are complete, peer-reviewed, and citable.

CrossRef is the innovative multi-publisher reference linking system enabling readers to move seamlessly from a reference in a journal article to the cited publication, typically located on a different server and published by a different publisher.

How can I access Wiley InterScience?

Visit http://www.interscience.wiley.com.

Guest Users can browse Wiley InterScience for unrestricted access to journal tables of contents and article abstracts, or use the powerful search engine.
Registered Users are provided with a *Personal Home Page* to store and manage customized alerts, searches, and links to favorite journals and articles. Additionally, Registered Users can view free online sample issues and preview selected material from major reference works.
Licensed Customers are entitled to access full-text journal articles in PDF, with select journals also offering full-text HTML.

How do I become an Authorized User?

Authorized Users are individuals authorized by a paying Customer to have access to the journals in Wiley InterScience. For example, a university that subscribes to Wiley journals is considered to be the Customer.
Faculty, staff, and students authorized by the university to have access to those journals in Wiley InterScience are Authorized Users. Users should contact their library for information on which Wiley journals they have access to in Wiley InterScience.

ASK YOUR INSTITUTION ABOUT WILEY INTERSCIENCE TODAY!